FOR THE
LOVE
⧉ OF ⧉
VEG

Hailing from North Wales, Bryn Williams learnt to appreciate food and its origins from an early age. Bryn has worked in some of the most prestigious kitchens in London. In 1997 he began work under Marco Pierre White at The Criterion, went on to work under Michel Roux Jr at Le Gavroche for three years, was senior-sous at The Orrery for four years and then moved to open Galvin at Windows with Chris Galvin. In 2006 he opened his own restaurant – Odette's – a neighbourhood favourite in London's Primrose Hill.

In 2006, Bryn won the first series of the Great British Menu on BBC1. His first book, *Bryn's Kitchen*, was published in 2011 and was nominated for the Jeremy Round Award for Best First Book at the 2012 Guild of Food Writers Awards. *Bryn's Kitchen* was the inspiration for his first TV series *Cegin Bryn* (Welsh for 'Bryn's Kitchen'). In addition, Bryn regularly appears on BBC1's *Saturday Kitchen* and has appeared on ITV's *This Morning*.

FOR THE
LOVE
≈ OF ≈
VEG

GET THE BEST OUT OF YOUR
SEASONAL FRUIT AND VEGETABLES

Bryn Williams

with Kay Plunkett-Hogge

Photography by Andy Sewell

Kyle Books

First published in Great Britain in 2013 by
Kyle Books
an imprint of Kyle Cathie Ltd
67–69 Whitfield Street
London, W1T 4HF
general.enquiries@kylebooks.com
www.kylebooks.com

10 9 8 7 6 5 4 3 2 1

ISBN: 978-0-85783-173-6

Project editors: Kyle Cathie and Catharine Robertson
Design: Aboud Creative
Photographer: Andy Sewell
Food stylist: Annie Rigg
Props stylist: Wei Tang
Copy editor: Stephanie Evans
Proofreader: Catherine Ward
Index: Lisa Footitt
Production: Nic Jones and David Hearn

A Cataloguing In Publication record for this title is available from the British Library.

Printed and bound in China by C&C Offset Printing Company Ltd.

CONTENTS

INTRODUCTION

Pretty much every young chef starts their career on the veg section. Scrubbing, peeling, trimming, chopping: it's one of the things we all have in common. And it's a key part of a culinary education – it's hard work, but you learn so much. It introduced me to incredible ingredients and it triggered my imagination, giving me a profound understanding of the produce beyond what I had learned growing up on a farm.

Looking back on more than 15 years in kitchens, I realise that all too often we take vegetables as dishes to be served on the side. We're all well aware of the different ways we can cook meat. We know that we can braise, roast, stew, grill, flash-fry, sear or sauté. And we know which cuts lend themselves to these different cooking techniques – most people, I hope, wouldn't try to pan-fry a beef shin or to slow-cook a tender fillet. But we often forget that it's just the same with fruit and vegetables. Different apples or potatoes or pumpkins lend themselves to being cooked in different ways. The simple cauliflower will benefit from our being a little more creative – there's more to be done with it than just boiling it or dousing it with cheese. It doesn't matter that vegetables seem more humble and are more affordable than turbot, which I love, or the finest piece of veal. Each vegetable demands the same care and attention we give to fish or meat.

I first learned this when I was barely 18, when I went to work at the one-starred Château Neercanne, near Maastricht in Holland. We used to do a dish with white asparagus. We had to measure out the right amount of water, to weigh out the salt and to boil the white asparagus for the exact amount of time, until it reached perfection. Even though I knew already all about the hard work the farmer puts into their growing, it was here I began to understand the proper respect we should give to vegetables in the kitchen.

It's this respect that forms the backbone of this book. Its recipes set out to show some love for our vegetables, and to redress the balance with the meat and fish, which so often are more prominent in our kitchens.

It is not a vegetarian book. Rather, it's a book about making the vegetables the stars of the show, not the sideshow. And it is a book that begins with two questions.

The first question is one I'm asked frequently by my customers at Odette's – what can I do with… They ask it for one of two reasons: either they have some celery or half a cucumber lurking in the back of the fridge, or they have a glut of tomatoes or apples in the garden. So I wanted to put together some recipes to help them out.

The second question came up after we'd cooked a supper club at the restaurant that focused three of its courses on game, before finishing with an apple tart with a Calvados cream. Could we, I wondered, host a supper club where we took one ingredient all the way through to the dessert as well? For that, we decided we had to lead with vegetables, ideally ones with a natural sweetness, which lend themselves to dessert. The supper clubs turned into events which really allowed these ingredients to shine. And those menus have become the heart of this book.

In *Bryn's Kitchen*, my first book, I talked about the hard work our farmers put into growing the vegetables we eat. I told stories about growing up on my uncle's farm, of planting and picking potatoes and beetroots, and of the relationship we have with the land, whether we're aware of it (and we should be) or not. And, as I did so, I realised how much we take vegetables for granted when we go to the shops. They're there in their plastic, often selected by supermarket buyers for their good looks rather than their flavour. We don't think about the six months of work that preceded our trip to the shops. We don't think about how the fields were ploughed and prepared, how the vegetable seedlings were fed and nurtured and finally planted out. And we don't think about how one bad summer can destroy the lot.

We're insulated from the sources of our food. But, rather than telling those stories once again, in this book I want to share the respect I gained for vegetables in the kitchen instead of on the land. And I want to demonstrate their versatility in terms of the flavours they offer us, and the range of cooking techniques that we can use for them.

Some of these techniques can be a little tricky. But there's one thing all the recipes have in common: when I cook a vegetable, I want to make sure you can really taste that vegetable in the finished dish. I want it to be able to stand up for itself on the plate, and to make sure that, whether I set it against meat or fish, its own flavours are not usurped or lost. I want to ensure that the vegetables are not simply a side dish or an after-thought, but that they are an equal part of the meal as a whole, and that, without them, something vital would be lost.

Let's get cooking.

VEGETABLES

MUSHROOM & TRUFFLE SUPPER CLUB

I love mushrooms. Anyone who has a copy of *Bryn's Kitchen* will know how I wax rhapsodic about them! Field mushrooms, button mushrooms, wild mushrooms all have their place in our kitchens and can add so much bosky, musky earthiness to dishes with their flavours and textures – and there is always one mushroom or another in season.

And yet, even with all those glorious ceps and girolles on our doorstep, I'll still choose simple button mushrooms or a meaty Portobello to cook with a steak on a Saturday night.

As for truffles, they really are nature's diamonds. The aroma is so intense, just a little goes a long way, so don't think you need to break the bank to experience the truffle's unique flavour – sometimes a little drop of infused oil is all that's needed.

As with all vegetables, you want to use the freshest mushrooms you can find. Where I grew up in Wales we had mushrooms all around us. But, apart from the field mushrooms, none of us knew what they were – and we didn't dare pick any! A lot of people are turning to mushroom-gathering to ensure they have the best. But, and this cannot be emphasised enough, unless you absolutely know what you're doing, don't gather mushrooms yourself: a lot of wild mushrooms have deadly lookalikes. Buy from the experts.

Clean mushrooms with a brush – avoid washing them in water if you can.

WHAT TO LOOK FOR:
- firm mushrooms that are unblemished and unbroken; avoid anything slimy or damp.

BAKED FIELD MUSHROOMS

Serves 4

Big, chunky, almost meaty field mushrooms – they are the ploughshare of the fungus world! Here, they are stuffed full of herby, mustardy butter and served alongside a light yet punchy parsley salad. I love these with a slice of toast in front of the rugby.

250g unsalted butter,
  softened
2 garlic cloves, crushed
1 shallot, peeled and
  finely chopped
1 tablespoon Dijon
  mustard
1 tablespoon chopped
  flat leaf parsley
8 large field mushrooms,
  stalks removed
salt and freshly ground
  black pepper

*for the shallot and
parsley salad:*
1 banana shallot, peeled
  and thinly sliced
bunch of flat leaf parsley,
  chopped
50ml Odette's House
  Dressing (see page 217)

Preheat the oven to 180°C/gas mark 4. Put the butter, garlic, shallot, Dijon mustard and parsley in a bowl. Season with salt and pepper and mix well together. Set aside.

Clean the mushrooms and place them, gill-side up, in a roasting tin. Top each one with a knob of the herb butter and bake in the oven for 7–10 minutes, depending on their size.

Mix together the ingredients for the salad. Season with salt and pepper to taste.

Serve the mushrooms with the salad on the side.

MORELS & LEMON SOLE

Serves 4

This is an Odette's classic. Throughout summer and into autumn, this is a winner. Madeira and morels are a match made in heaven and together they really bring out the delicate sweetness of the lemon sole.

4 lemon sole on the bone, trimmed and skinned

50ml vegetable oil

100g butter

1 shallot, peeled and finely chopped

200g fresh small morels, cleaned

sprig of thyme

150ml Madeira

150ml chicken stock

150ml double cream

salt and freshly ground black pepper

Season the sole with salt and pepper. Heat a large heavy-based frying pan over a medium heat. Add the vegetable oil. When it's hot, put in the sole and cook for 3–4 minutes. Add 50g of the butter and let it melt and foam up, then turn over the sole and cook for a further 3–4 minutes. Remove the fish from the pan, set aside and keep warm.

Return the cleaned frying pan to a medium heat. When it's hot, add the remaining butter. Allow it to melt, then add the shallot and cook without letting it colour. Then add the morels and the thyme, and cook for 2–3 minutes. Now add the Madeira and reduce by half. Pour in the stock, bring back to the boil and reduce by half. Then stir in the double cream – you're looking for it to turn the colour of café au lait. Bring back to the boil once more, season with salt and pepper and remove from the heat.

To serve, place a whole sole on a large plate and pour over the morel sauce. I like to serve this with steamed green asparagus when in season.

Bryn's Tip:
Don't be tempted to substitute red wine for the Madeira. Madeira is the ingredient that really brings this recipe alive. It goes perfectly with the morels. A red wine will just make the whole dish taste flat.

WHOLE ROASTED CEPS & RIB OF BEEF

Serves 2

This is a big, hearty, sexy dish – just imagine sharing it with the one you love.

---

2 ribs of beef on the bone,
  weighing 500g in total
3 tablespoons
  vegetable oil
800g firm cep mushrooms,
  cleaned
6 garlic cloves, peeled
  and thinly sliced
150g butter
handful of flat-leaf
  parsley, chopped
salt and freshly ground
  black pepper

Preheat the oven to 180°C/gas mark 4.

Season the beef generously with salt and pepper.

Place a heavy-based roasting tin (or a large heavy-based ovenproof frying pan) over a high heat. When it's hot, add 2 tablespoons of the vegetable oil and then the ribs. Cook until they are well sealed, about 3–4 minutes on each side. Do not rush this stage; the beef should be golden brown all over.

Put the ribs in the oven and roast for 10–12 minutes to serve medium-rare. Remove from the oven and set aside the beef to rest, covered, for 15 minutes, reserving the tray to roast the ceps.

Make 4 incisions into each cep with the point of a sharp knife. Push a slice of garlic into each incision. Then season the ceps with salt and pepper. Put the cleaned out roasting tray back over the heat. When the tray is hot, add the remaining vegetable oil, then tip in the ceps and cook for 2–3 minutes. Return the tray to the oven and bake for 10–15 minutes. Add the butter and the chopped parsley, and cook for a further 3–4 minutes or until the butter is golden (not burnt!).

Serve the ceps alongside the ribs, and don't forget to use the beef juices and the cep butter – I like to flood the plates with them!

TRUFFLE & PINEAPPLE CARPACCIO

Serves 4

How many of us have come back from holiday with a truffle in a jar of oil? Then it just gathers dust in the back of the cupboard... come on, own up! I know I have. This dish was inspired by that jar I brought back some while ago. The original idea dates from my time at The Orrery in Marylebone, London. The extreme, sweet stickiness of pineapple and the earthy, musky black truffle make for a distinctive and delicious end to a meal. You will have to start this the day before you want to serve it.

1 pineapple, peeled
500ml Stock Syrup
(see page 218)
sprig of lemon thyme,
leaves only
1 teaspoon chopped
black truffle
drop of truffle oil,
if you have any

Slice the pineapple as thinly as possible using a sharp knife, then put the slices in a single layer in a roasting tin.

Heat the stock syrup gently over a low heat, bringing it up to a simmer. Remove from the heat, add the lemon thyme, the truffle and the truffle oil, if using. Mix well. While the syrup is still warm, pour over the slices of pineapple. Cover with clingfilm and set aside to cool. Once completely cool, place the tin in the fridge to marinate overnight.

To serve, put the pineapple on a large plate and drizzle with the syrup, ensuring you include as much of the thyme and truffle as possible.

LEEKS

I don't recall eating a lot of leeks when I was a kid, even though the leek is synonymous with Wales. But it's hardly going to surprise anyone when I admit that I love them. In the restaurant, we often use them as a background flavour rather than making them a star player on their own, but they deserve to be centre stage a lot more. At home, I like to chop up a leek and then simply fry it in butter. Seasoned with salt and pepper, perhaps with a touch of curry powder (somehow this really brings out the flavour), this makes a lovely side dish. Baby leeks are perfect for stir-frying: trim them up, and bang them into a hot wok with some vegetable or sesame oil. Add a little soy sauce, and there you have it: pure perfection.

In some dishes leeks and onions can be used interchangeably but do remember that leeks are more subtly flavoured and delicate than onions.

Ensure your leeks are washed very thoroughly before using – soil or grit is easily trapped in the tight layers.

WHAT TO LOOK FOR:
* firm, unblemished white stems and bright green, sturdy tops.

LEEK & EGG SALAD

Serves 4

This is a Frenchified take on two very humble ingredients. Don't let the simplicity of this dish fool you: it is utterly delicious. Use only the white and pale green parts of the leek here: trim off the dark green tops and use them for stock.

4 new season's leeks, washed and trimmed
2 tablespoons olive oil
sprig of thyme, leaves only
celery salt
100ml Odette's House Dressing (see page 217)
4 free range eggs, soft boiled
bunch of chives, chopped
salt and freshly ground black pepper

Preheat the oven to 160°C/gas mark 3.

Lay the leeks on a large sheet of foil and sprinkle with the olive oil, thyme, celery salt and pepper. Seal the foil tightly, leaving some room in the parcel for the leeks to steam. Place in a roasting tin and bake in the oven for 8–10 minutes, or until the leeks are just cooked. Remove the leeks from the foil. Set aside and keep warm.

Pour the House Dressing into a small bowl. Peel the soft-boiled eggs and roughly chop them into small, bite-sized pieces, ensuring you keep all that lovely yolk. Add the eggs and chopped chives to the dressing and season with salt and pepper.

Cut the warm leeks in half lengthways and arrange on a large plate. Spoon over the dressing, distributing the egg evenly over the leeks.

This dish is best eaten while the leeks are still warm.

Bryn's Tip: When storing leeks in the fridge, make sure they are wrapped up well as their strong flavour can taint other foods.

LEEK & GOAT'S CHEESE QUICHE

Serves 6–8

Real men – and everyone else – love quiche! This is a popular dish on the menu at Odette's. You simply can't beat its soft, wobbly interior in a crisp pastry shell. Serve it in warm wedges with a green salad.

20g butter, plus extra
   for greasing
1 quantity of Shortcrust
   Pastry (see page 219)
2 leeks, washed
   and trimmed
1 teaspoon curry powder
   of your choice
6 free range eggs
700ml double cream
100g soft goat's cheese
salt and freshly ground
   black pepper

Grease a 23cm tart tin with a removable base.

Roll out the shortcrust pastry on a lightly floured surface and use it to line the tart tin. Leave to rest for 1 hour. Preheat the oven to 160°C/gas mark 3. Line the pastry shell with greaseproof paper and baking beans then bake blind for 25 minutes. Remove from the oven and lift off the paper and beans. Set the tart shell aside.

Cut the leeks in half lengthways, then slice them thinly. Melt the butter in a heavy-based saucepan over a medium heat, then add the leeks. Season with salt, pepper and curry powder and cook, without allowing the leeks to colour, until soft. Remove the pan from the heat and set aside.

Crack the eggs carefully into a large bowl and gently whisk in the double cream. Crumble in the goat's cheese and season with salt and pepper.

Transfer the cooked leeks to the pastry case. Pour in the egg mix and bake in the oven for 35–45 minutes or until cooked through and golden on top.

Serve slightly warm, or at room temperature.

ONIONS & SHALLOTS

When we cook, we quickly get used to using onions in dishes. Chopped onions form the base of so many sauces and stews. But I want to encourage people to think of onions as a main ingredient. And I'm not just talking about onion soup or fried onion rings.

As a chef, you quickly learn to appreciate the different types of onions and what they can do for your dishes. White onions from Italy, for example, are sweeter than many of those grown elsewhere; Spanish onions are large and sweet too – sometimes red in colour. Smaller yellow onions are the strongest, while shallots can vary in shape and size from tiny purple and pungent Thai ones to the more mellow banana variety. Our home-grown onions are different again, which some people put down to our northerly climate.

Sometimes, I think of onions as different hues of a primary colour, each adding a subtle and distinct dimension to a dish. When you single them out and cook them properly, you reveal not only their inherent sweetness, but their individuality as well.

WHAT TO LOOK FOR:
- no shrivelling – we want firm bulbs with tight skins and a nice regular sizing.
- don't touch anything that's sprouting!

ONION TART

This is my British version of the southern French classic, *pissaladière* – a delicious buttery pastry tart groaning with melted onions. Serve as a light lunch, a starter, or just to stave off any hunger pangs alongside a crisp glass of wine.

200ml olive oil, plus extra for greasing

1 quantity of Shortcrust Pastry (see page 219)

12 large onions, thinly sliced

sprig of rosemary, leaves only, chopped

salt

Preheat the oven to 180°C/gas mark 4 and grease a 23cm tart tin with a removable base.

Roll out the shortcrust pastry on a lightly floured surface and use it to line the tart tin. Leave a little excess pastry hanging over the lip of the tin to help the tart keep its shape. You can trim this when it's cooked. Line the pastry shell with greaseproof paper and baking beans then bake blind for 15–20 minutes. Remove from the oven and lift off the paper and beans. Set the tart shell aside.

Lower the oven temperature to 160°C/gas mark 3.

Place a very large saucepan over a medium heat. Add the olive oil and all of the sliced onions. Season with a pinch of salt, mix well, and cover with a lid. This will help to draw all the water from the onions. Leave for 5 minutes, then stir well and put the lid back on the saucepan. You will need to do this 3 or 4 times until the liquid has come out of the onions, and they soften in their juices without taking any colour.

Once the onions are soft, remove the lid and allow the liquid to evaporate, stirring all the time. Once the liquid starts to evaporate, and the onions begin to turn golden brown, add the chopped rosemary and continue to cook the onion until all the liquid has evaporated. This is very important: too much liquid means that when you put them into the tart case, the pastry will become soggy. When the onions are cooked, remove them from the saucepan and set aside to cool.

Transfer the cooled onions to the pastry case, then cook the tart in the oven for 20–25 minutes until the onion is really golden and has caramelised on top.

Serve at room temperature.

BRAISED ONIONS & SHOULDER OF LAMB

Serves 4–6

You know how good fried onions are with a hot dog or a steak? Well, this is just my grown-up way of having fried onions for Sunday lunch! The lovely little onions in this dish cook in the lamb fat, becoming so sweet and tender, while the balsamic vinegar adds a tang for balance.

1.5–2kg shoulder of lamb
20 baby onions or
   shallots, peeled
2 heads of garlic,
   unpeeled
500ml lamb stock
bunch of thyme
100ml good
   balsamic vinegar
salt and freshly ground
   black pepper

Preheat the oven to 160°C/gas mark 3. Score the lamb using a sharp knife then season it with salt and pepper. Put it in a roasting tin, and transfer to the oven for 40 minutes. Remove the tin from the oven and pour off any excess fat. Add the onions, garlic and stock, then put the tin back in the oven for 2 hours, basting the lamb every 30 minutes. After 2 hours, add the thyme and balsamic vinegar and continue to cook for a further 30 minutes.

Slice the lamb and serve with the onions and the cooking juices.

Bryn's Tip: You could just as easily use a joint of beef for this dish. Just alter the cooking times accordingly.

SHALLOT BREAD

Makes 2 loaves

We make this bread fresh every morning at Odette's. Try it warm from the oven, slathered with butter. This makes enough for 2 loaves: use one fresh and freeze the other for later.

45ml olive oil, plus extra
for greasing
4 shallots, peeled
and diced
sprig of thyme,
leaves only
15g fresh yeast
320ml lukewarm water
500g strong flour,
plus extra for dusting
2 teaspoons salt
20g onion powder
(optional)

Grease two 450g loaf tins. Put 1 tablespoon olive oil in a lidded pan over a medium heat and cook the shallots, covered, until soft. Remove the lid, add the thyme leaves and cook for a further 5 minutes until the shallots are golden brown. Set aside to cool.

Dissolve the yeast in the lukewarm water. Mix together all the dry ingredients in a large bowl with the remaining 30ml olive oil, and make a well in the centre using your hands. Then pour the yeast-infused water into it.

Gradually work the flour into the water, working gently with your fingertips until all the liquid has been absorbed, and you have a cohesive dough. It should feel smooth, not crumbly or ragged. If it does feel crumbly, add a spoonful more water.

Turn out the dough onto a well-floured surface and knead it for a good 5 minutes. The feel you are after is smooth, silky and elastic, and it should look shiny. Put the dough into a clean bowl, cover with a damp cloth and leave to rise in a warm place for 30–40 minutes.

When the dough has doubled in size, use your fists to knock back or punch down the dough into the bowl – do this a couple of times to remove any air pockets and help with the texture of the bread. Then add the cooled shallot to the dough and mix well.

Preheat the oven to 180°C/gas mark 4.

Turn out the dough onto a floured surface and split the mix into equal halves. Knead each one and shape into 2 loaves. Place the loaves into the prepared tins, and leave them in a warm place to rise for about 30 minutes, or until doubled in size. Bake in the oven for 35–40 minutes.

Remove from the oven and set aside to cool for 10 minutes before removing the loaves from their tins. Serve as fresh as possible.

Bryn's Tip: I really encourage you to use fresh yeast – it makes all the difference, and the smell and feel are just wonderful. But if you are using easy-blend dried yeast, just follow the instructions on the packet, and you will be fine.

SHALLOT CHUTNEY

Makes about 1 litre

This is a staple in my store cupboard. Fruity, spicy and sweet. I love it with terrines, cold meats and cheese.

1kg shallots, peeled
    and sliced
500g Braeburn apples,
    peeled, cored
    and grated
100g raisins
2 tablespoons
    mustard seeds
1 teaspoon
    ground ginger
450ml white wine vinegar
300g brown sugar

Place all the ingredients in a large, lidded heavy-based pan and bring to the boil. Cover the pan and simmer until the shallots are soft – about 20 minutes.

Uncover the pan and continue to cook until the mixture has thickened nicely. This should take another 20 minutes or so.

Remove from the heat and ladle into clean jars, sterilised by following the method on page 220.

CELERIAC

Celeriac may not be the most beautiful vegetable at the ball, but don't let that put you off. Once you get past its slightly hairy, gnarled exterior it is delicious, tasting like a softer, creamier version of celery, which is hardly surprising since it is, basically, an edible celery root. There's so much you can do with it! You can use it raw, baked, or roasted, and it makes a silky, sexy soup. With this one, beauty really does lie within. With the recipes here, I'm trying to showcase some of celeriac's versatility. But if you really want to serve it at its purest, peel it carefully, cut it into chunks, and bake it, covered with a layer of sea salt in the oven preheated to 170°C/gas mark 3 for about 25 minutes. Then, when it's cooked, wipe off the salt and serve. Cooked like this, celeriac is earthy and comforting, and perfect with a rare piece of venison.

WHAT TO LOOK FOR:
- celeriac should feel heavy for its size.
- this root often has a better flavour in the cooler months.

CELERIAC & APPLE SOUP

Serves 4

Earthy, autumnal flavours abound in this soothing soup. The mellow celeriac is perked up nicely by the sharp-sweet apple. Serve with crusty bread.

50g butter
1 shallot, peeled
  and sliced
sprig of thyme,
  leaves only
3 Braeburn apples,
  peeled, cored and sliced
1 medium celeriac,
  peeled and diced into
  2cm cubes
1 litre good vegetable
  stock
300ml double cream
salt and freshly ground

Melt the butter in a large heavy-based saucepan over a gentle heat without allowing it to colour. Add the shallot and the thyme leaves and sweat gently for about 4–5 minutes or until the shallot is soft. Add the apple and the celeriac and sweat for a further 7–8 minutes. Season the celeriac mixture with salt and pepper to taste.

Add the stock to the saucepan and bring it to the boil. Simmer for 10–12 minutes then add the cream. Bring back to the boil. Remove from the heat and whizz with an immersion blender until it's nice and smooth.

Pass the soup through a fine sieve and serve in warm bowls.

BAKED CELERIAC & CRISPY DUCK EGG SALAD

Serves 4

Here we set creamy, smooth, baked celeriac against the crunchy crumb exterior and runny richness of duck egg. It is another match made in heaven.

4 duck eggs
100g plain flour
2 free range eggs,
  lightly beaten
100g breadcrumbs
1 medium celeriac,
  peeled but left whole
2 tablespoons vegetable
  oil, plus extra for
  deep-frying
50g butter
2 sprigs of thyme
100ml Truffle Vinaigrette
  (see page 216)
sea salt and freshly
  ground black pepper
handful of celery leaves,
  to garnish

Place the duck eggs in boiling salted water for 6 minutes. Drain, then put them in ice-cold water for 30 minutes.

Peel the duck eggs carefully. Roll them in the flour, then in the lightly beaten eggs, and finally in the breadcrumbs. Place the coated eggs on a baking tray and transfer them to the fridge.

Preheat the oven to 180°C/gas mark 4.

Season the celeriac with salt and pepper.

Heat a large, heavy-based, ovenproof frying pan over a low to medium heat. Add the vegetable oil followed by the whole celeriac, and colour it all over. This should take about 6–7 minutes in all, so be a little patient. You will need to rest the celeriac on the side of the frying pan as you turn it to ensure it develops a nice even, golden brown colour all over.

When the celeriac is coloured, add the butter and the thyme to the frying pan then transfer it to the oven, and bake for 20 minutes. Baste the celeriac with the butter 2–3 times as it cooks. When it's ready – a knife should slide into it easily – remove from the oven, and set aside on a plate to cool.

When cool enough to handle, cut the celeriac as thinly as possible. Place the slices on a plate or a baking tray and season with the truffle vinaigrette and sea salt.

Heat the oil in a deep-fat fryer to 180°C.

Deep-fry the eggs straight from the fridge for 1 minute or until the breadcrumbs are golden brown.

To serve, place slices of celeriac on a large plate. Try to create some height and texture with them. Cut off the top of the eggs to reveal the runny yolk and place the eggs in the middle of the celeriac. Then scatter the celery leaves over the dish before serving.

CELERIAC REMOULADE & MACKEREL

Serves 4

Classic French remoulade meets a favourite British fish – it's *entente cordiale* in a dish. Setting the horseradish-spiked crunch of the celeriac remoulade against the silky, fatty, rich mackerel gives you wonderful flavour and mouth-feel, making this a terrific starter or light lunch.

1 medium celeriac
juice of 1 lemon
200g Mayonnaise
  (see the Herb
  Mayonnaise recipe
  on page 77, and omit
  the herbs)
2 tablespoons
  creamed horseradish
vegetable oil, for greasing
4 mackerel fillets
chervil and chives,
  to garnish
salt and freshly ground
  black pepper

Peel the celeriac and cut into even slices about 3mm thick. Then cut the slices again into strips 3mm wide to create ribbons. Put the celeriac ribbons into a large bowl, add a pinch of salt and the lemon juice and mix well. Then tip the celeriac into a colander set over a bowl and leave to stand for 1 hour.

Using a clean kitchen cloth, squeeze out any excess water from the celeriac, then transfer the ribbons to a clean bowl, add the mayonnaise and the horseradish and stir together to bind.

Oil a fairly deep-sided baking tray and season it well with salt and pepper. Place the mackerel fillets on it, flesh-side down, and put the tray under a hot grill until they are cooked, say about 2–3 minutes. Try to ensure the mackerel flesh stays slightly pink in the middle.

For each portion, place a spoon of the celeriac on a cold plate and accompany with a mackerel fillet. Finish with the fresh herbs.

CELERY

A lot of people only buy celery when they plan to serve Bloody Marys! Or it is used as a shovel for cream cheese and dips, or as a garnish for the cheese board along with a few grapes. And the rest of it sits in the corner of the vegetable drawer in the fridge until it wilts to oblivion. It deserves to come in from the cold!

Celery has a vital role to play in the kitchen. It is indispensable as a base for stocks and sauces, and as a keynote flavour in stews and stuffings. Used raw it adds a pleasing crunch to dishes, and assumes a silky texture when cooked. And, if you treat it kindly, it's delicious in its own right. So it's time to reach into the back of the fridge and set it free.

WHAT TO LOOK FOR:
• tightly packed heads, firm sticks, fresh, bright green leaves and a sound base.

CELERY & BLUE CHEESE SOUP

Serves 4

We are more used to this combination being served as part of a cheese course, with the crisp raw celery being brought out at the end of a meal with wedges of rich blue cheese. Here we have turned the combination on its head to make a hot and delicious soup. I love to use Perl Las, a Welsh blue cheese, but you can use any blue cheese you like as long as it's not too salty.

50g butter
1 onion, peeled
   and chopped
1 teaspoon fennel seeds
1 head of celery,
   trimmed and chopped,
   leaves reserved
1 litre good chicken or
   vegetable stock
300g double cream
200g blue cheese
salt and freshly ground
   black pepper

Melt the butter in a large saucepan and add the onion and fennel seeds. Sweat for 4–5 minutes until the onion is soft. Add the celery and sweat for another 7–8 minutes until the celery starts to soften. Season with salt and pepper.

Add the stock, bring to the boil then simmer for 5–6 minutes. Add the cream and bring back to the boil. Stir in the blue cheese, then remove the pan from the heat. Transfer the contents to a blender or food-processor – remember, it will be very hot – and whizz until smooth. Pass through a fine sieve into a clean saucepan or bowl, and reheat gently if necessary.

To serve, pour the soup into bowls and garnish with the reserved celery leaves. If you have any blue cheese left over, scatter a little on top of each bowl.

BRAISED CELERY & POACHED BRILL

Serves 4

Braising celery really brings out its flavour, giving it a beautifully soft yet toothsome texture. Brill, a firm white fish – in terms of flavour, think of it as one step down from turbot – is more than able to stand up to celery and also to take on all those wonderful herby flavours from the poaching liquid.

2 whole heads of celery,
  with the leaves
2 tablespoons
  vegetable oil
150ml dry white wine
500ml good chicken stock
1 sprig of thyme
2 bay leaves
6 black peppercorns
zest of 1 lemon
4 x 160g pieces of brill or
  1 whole brill, cleaned,
  trimmed and filleted
salt and freshly ground
  black pepper

to garnish:
large handful of parsley,
  leaves only
reserved celery leaves

Preheat the oven to 140°C/gas mark 1.

Trim the celery stalks to around 12cm from the base of the celery heart, keeping all the remaining celery to make soup or vegetable stock, and setting the leaves aside for garnishing the finished dish. Now cut the celery hearts lengthways into quarters.

Season the celery with salt and pepper. Place a large roasting tin over a medium heat. Add the vegetable oil, then put the celery into the warmed tin and cook for a few minutes, just to give it a little colour. Add the white wine and stock. Bring to a simmer, add the thyme, bay leaves, peppercorns and the lemon zest. Then transfer the tin to the oven for 30–40 minutes, or until the celery is tender.

Remove the celery from the liquid using a slotted spoon. Set aside to keep warm. Place the roasting tin back on the hob, put the brill into the liquid and poach over a medium heat for 5–6 minutes, or until just cooked.

To serve, place the celery hearts into warm bowls, put the brill on top, and pour some of the cooking liquid around it. Finish with the celery and parsley leaves.

CARROT SUPPER CLUB

Too many people look at carrots as something of a one-trick pony. Often you'll just find them turned and simply boiled. But there's so much you can do with a carrot! Beyond their important role in stocks and stews, they can be grated, roasted, pickled, sautéed, you name it. They take flavour well, and sit comfortably with spices – just think of carrot cake. But you really need to hunt out the good ones. All too frequently, we buy carrots in sealed plastic, which means they've been chosen for their smoothness and perfect straightness, and they've been left to sweat out their flavour in the bags. Again, I urge you to buy from farmers' markets or vegetable clubs when you can. All your veg will taste better for it, but the difference is especially noticeable with carrots. A good carrot is sweet, crisp and full of juicy goodness. And don't forget, orange carrots are a fairly new invention – they were cross-bred to honour a Dutch king. With purple and white carrots now becoming more readily available as farmers rediscover heritage varieties, you get the opportunity to try something that's both old and new at the same time, and to add some welcome colour to the plate.

WHAT TO LOOK FOR:
- firm carrots with bright colour.
- bright green and perky leaves (if still attached).

CARROT & BLOOD ORANGE SALAD

Serves 4–6

The colours of this salad alone are enough to wake up the most jaded palate. The sweetness of the carrot, the sharpness of the orange and the chalky saltiness of the goat's cheese come together to create a cloud-flecked sunrise on a plate.

12 medium carrots, peeled
3 blood oranges
pinch of sugar
50ml white wine vinegar
200ml olive oil
100g soft goat's cheese
bunch of watercress,
    washed
salt and freshly ground
    black pepper

Slice the carrots lengthways as thinly as possible, using a mandolin. Put them into a bowl of iced water to keep them crisp.

Peel the blood oranges using a sharp knife, then segment all 3 oranges, ensuring you catch all the juice – it's best to do this over a bowl. To make the dressing, put the juice and the segments from 1 orange into a separate bowl. Add the sugar and whisk together until the segments are broken down. Pour in the vinegar and the olive oil and whisk again, then season with salt and pepper to taste.

Drain and dry the carrots thoroughly, then place them in a clean bowl. Drizzle with the blood orange dressing, add the segments from the remaining 2 blood oranges and mix carefully, trying not to break the segments.

To serve, arrange the dressed carrot and blood orange salad onto a large plate, crumble the goat's cheese over it, and finish with the watercress. Drizzle any remaining dressing over the top.

PICKLED CARROTS & MACKEREL

Serves 4

Agrodolce or sour-sweet carrots with notes of woody spice are a perfect counterpoint to oil-rich mackerel and cut through its fattiness. It's my light and very British version of escabeche.

300ml white wine vinegar
150ml white wine
250g sugar
1 teaspoon coriander
   seeds
2 bay leaves
2 star anise
sprig of thyme
6 medium carrots,
   peeled and sliced 50ml
olive oil, plus extra for
   greasing
4 mackerel fillets
sprig of coriander,
   chopped
salt and freshly ground
   black pepper

Put the vinegar, wine and sugar into a large saucepan and bring to the boil. Add the coriander seeds, bay leaves, star anise and thyme, and bring to the boil. Add the sliced carrots, bring back to the boil, then remove the pan from the heat immediately. Set aside.

Oil a fairly deep-sided baking tray and season it well with salt and pepper. Place the mackerel fillets on it, flesh-side down, and put the tray under a hot grill until they are cooked, say about 2–3 minutes. Try to ensure the mackerel flesh stays slightly pink in the middle. Set aside to keep warm.

Remove the carrots from the vinegar using a slotted spoon or tongs and transfer to a bowl. Season with salt and pepper. Add the olive oil and the coriander to the vinegar mixture and stir well.

To serve, place the pickled carrots next to the mackerel and drizzle the dressing around it.

CONFIT CARROT & PORK BELLY

Serves 4–6

Here you are essentially using the same method – confiting – to cook both the pork and the carrots, the difference being that the pork will render and become soft and sticky while the carrot will maintain its firmness and get sweeter. You may need to start this dish the day before you want to serve it.

for the confit of carrot:
1kg duck fat
1 star anise
2 cardamom pods,
   lightly crushed
sprig of thyme
6 peppercorns
8 whole carrots, peeled
   with some of the green
   top left on

for the pork belly:
1kg pork belly
2 tablespoons olive oil
salt and freshly ground
   black pepper

Pour the duck fat into a saucepan large enough to fit all the carrots. Add the star anise, cardamom pods, thyme and the peppercorns, and place the pan over a low heat. Add the carrots and cook for 1 hour or until just tender – the duck fat should never boil. When ready, leave the carrots to cool in the duck fat and set aside in the fridge until needed.

Preheat the oven to 140°C/gas mark 1.

Rub the pork belly thoroughly with 1 tablespoon of the olive oil, and then season well with salt and pepper. Place it in a good-sized roasting tin and put it in the oven for 5–6 hours, until melting and tender.

Remove from the oven and transfer to a clean roasting tin. Place another tin on top of the pork and weigh it down (I often use unopened cans from the store cupboard) – you want to keep the shape of the pork. Let it cool, and then put the whole thing into the fridge until completely cold; overnight is fine.

When you are ready to serve, remove the skin from the pork belly (see tip). Cut the belly into slices 2cm thick and season with salt and pepper. Heat the remaining tablespoon of olive oil in a frying pan over a medium heat, and gently fry the slices until they are golden brown on both sides. Remove and set aside to keep warm.

Take the carrots out of the duck fat and place them into the same frying pan. Season with salt and pepper and heat through until warm.

I like to serve this with some of my Shallot Chutney (see page 34).

Bryn's Tips: Instead of discarding the skin, why not make some pork scratchings? Cut the pork skin into finger-sized pieces. Ensure the skin is dried THOROUGHLY. Heat some oil in a deep-fat fryer to 180°C and deep-fry the skin until crispy. Remove, set aside on kitchen paper to drain and serve sprinkled with sea salt.

In the restaurant, we measure out a litre of duck fat for this, but since it's easier to buy it by weight in the shops, I have listed it that way here.

CARROT CAKE

Serves 8–10

Everyone loves carrot cake. The natural sweetness and succulence of carrots make them perfect for adding to desserts. We can actually trace the roots of the carrot cakes we eat today back to 10th-century Arabic recipes for spiced carrot puddings and sweetmeats. Once a good thing, always a good thing!

400g caster sugar
290ml vegetable oil
4 free range eggs
370g plain flour
1½ teaspoons baking
  powder
1 tablespoon ground
  cinnamon
1 teaspoon salt
480g coarsely grated
  carrot (about 500g
  unpeeled carrots)

Preheat the oven to 160°C/gas mark 3. Line a 28 x 20cm rectangular cake tin with greaseproof paper.

Mix together the sugar and the oil in a large bowl until well combined. Stir in the eggs then fold in the dry ingredients. Mix thoroughly. Add the grated carrot and stir again until well combined.

Carefully spoon the mixture into the prepared tin and bake in the oven for 20 minutes or until golden brown and firm to the touch. The surface should spring back when you press it gently with your finger.

Remove the cake from the oven and allow it to cool in the tin.

Serve cut into squares.

PARSNIP SUPPER CLUB

The parsnip's natural sweetness, which I often like to enhance with honey, lends itself to desserts more easily than you'd expect, so it seemed from the outset to be a very good choice for the Supper Clubs. For generations people have been using parsnips to add sweetness to food when sugar was scarce. One of my favourite stories is about mums in the Second World War using parsnips to make faux banana sandwiches by mashing up boiled parsnips, then adding a little colour and some flavouring, if they could get it. Genius!

In addition to their sweetness, parsnips offer an earthy, warming note, which makes them a fantastic winter vegetable. They store well, and help us to get through the cold months when little is growing until the greens reappear in the spring. But whereas different varieties of potatoes offer up different culinary options, the different types of parsnip seem to exist more to adapt the plant to variable growing conditions and soil types. A word of warning if you want to grow parsnips yourself: the leaves are not edible. In fact, they can give you a nasty rash when you touch them, so always wear gloves when you handle them.

WHAT TO LOOK FOR:
- firm, unblemished and medium-sized roots.
- bright green and perky leaves (if still attached).
- avoid broken parsnips or those that feel spongy.

PARSNIP & CHESTNUT SOUP

Serves 4–6

Autumn breezes and rust-hued leaves are evoked with this luxurious soup.

50g butter
600g parsnips, peeled
   and chopped
1 small leek, trimmed
   and chopped
150ml white wine
200g cooked chestnuts
   (sold vacuum-packed),
   plus a few extra to
   garnish
1½ litres good
   vegetable stock
salt and freshly ground
   black pepper

Melt the butter in a large heavy-based saucepan over a gentle heat but do not allow it to colour. Add the parsnips and leek and let them sweat gently for about 4–5 minutes or until the parsnip is soft. Add the white wine and chestnuts and sweat for a further 7–8 minutes. Season the mixture with salt and pepper to taste.

Add the stock to the saucepan and bring to the boil then simmer for 5–6 minutes. Remove the pan from the heat and blend with an immersion blender or in a food-processor until it's nice and smooth. (If you're using a food-processor, allow the soup to cool a little before you whizz it.)

Pass the soup through a fine sieve and serve in warm bowls with the extra chestnuts crumbled on top.

PARSNIP MASH & PAN-FRIED SALMON

Serves 4

This is visually a stunner – pale pink salmon resting on a creamy cushion of parsnips. The salmon has the strength and structure to take on the punchy horseradish and the sweet parsnip, making this a wonderful winter supper dish too.

50g butter
5 large parsnips,
    peeled and chopped
100ml water
1 tablespoon
    creamed horseradish
4 x 175g salmon supremes
1 tablespoon
    vegetable oil
juice of ½ lemon
salt and freshly ground
    black pepper

Melt the butter in a large, lidded heavy-based saucepan over a medium heat and add the parsnips. Season with salt and pepper. Add the water, then cover the pan and slowly cook for 10–15 minutes until the parsnips are tender and there is no remaining water.

When the parsnips are cooked, remove the lid and add the horseradish. Boil for 1 minute then mash using a potato masher or the back of a fork. Set aside and keep warm.

Season the salmon with salt and pepper. Heat the oil in a frying pan over a medium heat. Add the salmon and cook for 3–4 minutes on one side then turn over and cook for 1 minute. Remove the pan from the heat and add the lemon juice.

To serve, spoon the parsnip mash into warm bowls or plates and place the salmon on top.

HONEY-ROASTED PARSNIP
& DUCK BREAST

Serves 4

This dish merges two schools of flavour I came across in my early cheffing years: the Asian staple of soy and honey coupled with the honey and rosemary parsnips we used to cook at Le Gavroche. Fatty, crisp duck breasts sit so well within the framework.

---

4 duck breasts, skin on
100ml vegetable oil
6 large parsnips, peeled
    and cut into 6 batons
50g unsalted butter
3 tablespoons honey
couple of sprigs of
    rosemary, leaves
    stripped and
    coarsely chopped
splash of soy sauce
salt and freshly ground
    black pepper

Preheat the oven to 160°C/gas mark 3.

Score the skin of the duck with a sharp knife, then season with salt and pepper. Place an ovenproof frying pan over a medium heat. When it is hot, put the breasts skin-side down into the pan. Leave until the skin has browned, then turn them over and seal the flesh. Turn them back onto their skin side, and transfer the pan to the oven. Roast for 10–12 minutes. Remove the breasts from the pan and set aside to rest, covered in tin foil, while you prepare the parsnips.

Wipe out the pan or select a second, large, ovenproof frying pan. Place over a medium heat and add the vegetable oil. When it is hot, add the parsnips. Sauté for 4–5 minutes, then add the butter. Cook until the butter has melted, then drizzle in the honey. Transfer the pan to the oven and bake for 8–10 minutes but keep an eye on it – you don't want the honey to burn. When it's ready, remove from the oven, add the chopped rosemary then pour in the soy sauce and mix well.

Slice the duck onto individual plates (or keep whole if you prefer) and serve the parsnips alongside.

PARSNIP ICE CREAM & WARM CHOCOLATE CAKE

Serves 4

Unusual as it may sound, parsnip ice cream has been around in one form or another for a while now. The secret is not to make it too overpowering. The contrast of the sweet, milky and uniquely fragrant ice cream with the rich, dark cake is a modern twist on a classic dessert pairing.

for the ice cream:
4 free range egg yolks
100g caster sugar
200g parsnips, peeled and finely chopped
500ml milk
350ml double cream

for the chocolate cake:
250g good-quality dark chocolate, minimum 70% cocoa solids
200g unsalted butter
5 free range eggs
4 free range egg yolks
125g caster sugar
2 tablespoons plain flour

Start with the ice cream. Whisk the egg yolks and sugar together in a large bowl and set aside.

Put the parsnips in a large saucepan. Pour over the milk and the cream, bring to the boil and simmer gently until the parsnip is cooked.

Remove the parsnip mixture from the heat and while still hot, pour it over the egg and sugar mixture, whisking all the time until combined. Pour everything back into the pan and heat gently, stirring all the time, until it is thick enough to coat the back of a spoon. Pass the mixture through a fine sieve into a clean bowl. Leave to cool completely before chilling in the fridge until cold.

Pour the chilled mixture into an ice-cream machine and churn until frozen, but not too stiff. Put the ice cream into a container and freeze for at least 1½ hours or until you are ready to use. Remember to transfer your ice cream from the freezer to the fridge about 20 minutes before you want to eat it.

To make the cake, put the chocolate and the unsalted butter in a heatproof bowl over a saucepan of barely simmering water, and stir occasionally until it's completely melted. Remove the bowl from the heat and set aside to cool slightly.

Beat the eggs, extra yolks and sugar in a large bowl, gently but thoroughly – you don't want too many air bubbles in this. Pour the melted chocolate mixture into the eggs and stir well to combine, and then gently fold in the flour. Tap the bowl on the work surface at this point, just to remove any air bubbles from the mixture. Pour the mixture carefully into 4 ovenproof ramekins or bowls. Put them in the fridge to chill for at least 30 minutes. You could leave them longer – even overnight if you want.

When you're ready to cook them, preheat the oven to 160°C/gas mark 3 and pop in the chilled ramekins for 6–8 minutes. When they're ready, remove from the oven, and top each warm pudding with a scoop of the ice cream.

ASPARAGUS

When locally grown asparagus comes in, you know that summer's just around the corner. It's one of those vegetables that people really look forward to. If you ever get the chance to have asparagus on the day it is picked, you're in for a treat: you can taste the natural sugars and the stalks are crisper and sweeter than ever.

If you can find fresh white asparagus – what the Dutch call 'white gold' – you could replicate a dish that I used to eat when I was a young lad, training at a hotel in Maastricht: simply steamed and covered in slices of ham and melted butter, with sieved boiled egg yolk sprinkled on top. Delicious.

Chefs generally try to cook asparagus as simply as possible because, although it has such a distinct flavour, it's one that's very easy to lose if you're careless. And the season is so short, you just want to make the asparagus the main event. That said, asparagus lends itself to simplicity. There's nothing sexier than an asparagus spear, freshly dipped in melted butter or hollandaise. Prep it, peel it if necessary, then roast, grill or boil it quickly and serve it at once.

WHAT TO LOOK FOR:
- firm, crisp tips that are tightly furled and sturdy stalks with no discoloration.
- try to make sure the stalks are not woody and dry.
- try to buy asparagus spears of an even size.

CHILLED ASPARAGUS & GARLIC MAYONNAISE

Serves 4

When asparagus comes into season, it starts – hopefully – to get warm outside. Which makes this a perfect light starter to enjoy al fresco.

28 asparagus spears

for the garlic mayonnaise:
2 free range egg yolks
2 garlic cloves, crushed
pinch of saffron
150ml vegetable oil

Cut off the hard portion of the asparagus stalks, then peel about 2cm from the base of each one. Tie the spears into bundles of 7 with kitchen string. This is so that each portion of 7 spears will be cooked uniformly. Cook the asparagus in boiling salted water for 4–6 minutes or until tender. Then remove from the heat, and place into ice-cold water to stop the cooking process and to keep the colour. When cold, remove the spears from the water, untie each bundle and set aside on kitchen paper to dry.

Blend the egg yolks, garlic and saffron with a pinch of salt in a blender. With the

2 tablespoons dry
   mashed potato
150ml olive oil, plus 1
   tablespoon to dress
   the asparagus
lemon juice, to taste
salt and freshly ground
   black pepper

machine still running, slowly add the vegetable oil until it emulsifies and thickens to a nice mayonnaise consistency. Add the dry mashed potato and blend until smooth, then gradually add the olive oil to finish. If it's too thick, let it down with a little warm water, a spoonful at a time. Correct the seasoning with salt and lemon juice to taste.

To serve, place the asparagus in a large bowl and season with sea salt, pepper and a little olive oil. Arrange 7 asparagus spears on each plate, and spoon the garlic mayonnaise to the side.

WARM ASPARAGUS & WILD GARLIC HOLLANDAISE

Serves 4

Come late spring and early summer, you will always find this dish on the menu at Odette's – just-cooked spears and richly scented, glossy hollandaise.

for the garlic hollandaise:
200ml white wine vinegar
10 white peppercorns,
   crushed
sprig of thyme
1 bay leaf
250g unsalted butter
5 free range egg yolks
freshly squeezed lemon
   juice, to taste
12 wild garlic leaves,
   chopped
salt and freshly ground
   black pepper

28 asparagus spears

Put the vinegar into a saucepan with the crushed peppercorns, thyme and bay leaf, bring to the boil then simmer until it has reduced by half. Remove from the heat, and set aside to cool.

Melt the butter in another saucepan over a low heat until it foams, spoon off the foam and leave the butter to settle. Remove the clarified butter with a ladle, discarding the white residue at the bottom of the pan.

Put the egg yolks with 2 tablespoons of the reduced vinegar in a heatproof bowl over a pan of simmering water and whisk until light and creamy. Ensure the water does not touch the bowl, otherwise it will get too hot and scramble the eggs.

Remove from the heat, whisking continuously, and slowly pour in the clarified butter. Pass through a fine sieve, and season with salt and pepper, a squeeze of lemon juice, and the chopped wild garlic leaves.

Now prepare the asparagus: cut off the hard portion of the stalk, then peel about 2cm off the bottom of the asparagus and tie the spears into bundles of 7 with kitchen string. This is so that each portion of 7 spears will be cooked uniformly. Cook the asparagus in boiling salted water for 4–6 minutes or until tender.

Untie each bundle and arrange on plates, then pour over the hollandaise and serve.

Bryn's Tip: This makes a lot of reduced vinegar but, bottled and labelled, it will keep for up to 6 months in the fridge or until you make the sauce again.

LETTUCE

I know it's old-fashioned, but I love a wedge of Iceberg lettuce. Served with a healthy slug of Odette's House Dressing (see page 217), it's one of my favourite ways to start a meal. My uncle used to grow Icebergs and we ate them a lot in Wales when I was growing up – so maybe that's where it comes from.

There is a huge array of lettuce varieties out there, ranging from the commonly available floppy, round lettuce and crisp, sweet Baby Gems, which are great for cooking, to Cos and Romaine, which are great for Caesar Salad (like the one opposite) and dipping as they hold their shape. Then you have Frisée, Oak Leaf, Mesclun… the list goes on.

I never really cooked with lettuce until I started training to be a chef in Holland and France. There I learnt that lettuce is not just for salad. When it's a little past its best (or, if you'll excuse me, when its salad days are done), it's perfect for a braise or a soup. It was a useful thing to learn, because lettuces are not only easy to grow, they're a plant that just keeps on giving. Lots of gardeners end up with gluts of them, so it's good to have an extra few culinary options up your sleeve.

WHAT TO LOOK FOR:
• firm, crisp, bright green leaves.

CAESAR SALAD

Serves 4

It wasn't until I worked for Marco Pierre White at The Criterion that I realised what an extraordinary dish this is. It's not just a salad, it's a meal, and a real classic: something that requires care and attention to get right. It's all about the dressing… so please, take the time to get it right. It will be worth it.

for the dressing:
2 free range egg yolks
3 teaspoons white
   wine vinegar
1 teaspoon wholegrain
   mustard
50g grated Parmesan
   cheese
3 garlic cloves,
   finely chopped
8 anchovy fillets,
   cut into small pieces
pinch of salt
1 teaspoon
   Worcestershire sauce
125ml olive oil

for the salad:
2 large slices of white
   bread, for croûtons
2–3 tablespoons olive oil
2 medium Cos lettuce,
   separated into whole
   leaves, washed and
   dried thoroughly
4 anchovy fillets
Parmesan cheese shavings
salt and freshly ground
   black pepper

Preheat the oven to 180°C/gas mark 4.

First, make the dressing. Using a food-processor with a whisk attachment, whisk the egg yolks, vinegar, wholegrain mustard, grated Parmesan, garlic, anchovies, salt and Worcestershire sauce together. With the machine still running, slowly start to add the olive oil to the mix until it combines into a glossy emulsion, a little like mayonnaise. Set aside.

Dice the bread for the croûtons. Season with salt and pepper and roll in the olive oil. Spread them out on a baking tray and bake in the oven until golden brown, about 3–4 minutes. Remove from the oven and set aside to cool.

To serve, gently toss the lettuce leaves with the dressing, then transfer to a serving bowl, scatter the croûtons around and place the anchovy fillets on top, along with the Parmesan shavings.

BRAISED BABY GEM & ROAST CHICKEN

Serves 4–6

Braising these lovely little lettuces brings another texture and an incredible sweetness to a vegetable that is too often just torn up and tossed in a salad. Roast chicken is the perfect partner for a fresh take on a midweek supper.

1 whole chicken, weighing about 1.5kg
2 bay leaves
3 sprigs of thyme
50ml vegetable oil
1 head of garlic, broken into cloves, skin on
4 Baby Gem lettuces, trimmed, outer leaves removed if necessary
50g butter
1 small onion, peeled and diced
1 small carrot, peeled and diced
150ml Madeira
500ml good vegetable stock
salt and freshly ground black pepper

Preheat the oven to 180°C/gas mark 4.

Season the cavity of the chicken with salt. Place the bird in a large, heavy-based saucepan. Add the bay leaves and 2 of the thyme sprigs and pour in enough water to just cover the chicken. Place the pan over a high heat and bring to the boil. Remove it immediately from the heat and leave the chicken to cool in the pan for 10 minutes. Then lift the chicken from the water and set aside on a wire rack to dry thoroughly. Discard the cooking liquor – or turn it into stock if you wish.

While the chicken is drying, place a roasting tin in the oven to get hot, for about 10 minutes or so. Season the chicken generously with salt and pepper, and drizzle with 1 tablespoon of the vegetable oil. Put the garlic in a small bowl, season with salt and pepper and add the rest of the vegetable oil.

Remove the tin from the oven. Place the chicken in the middle and scatter the garlic cloves around it, reserving the oil. Roast in the oven for 40–50 minutes or until the skin is golden and the juices run clear.

Cut the Baby Gems in half lengthways. Heat the reserved vegetable oil in a large, heavy-based frying pan over a medium heat. Season the lettuce halves with salt and pepper, then place flat-side down in the pan and cook until golden brown. Remove from the pan and set aside.

Reduce the heat under the pan, add the butter, onion, carrot and remaining thyme sprig and season with salt and pepper. Sweat the vegetables for 2–3 minutes, then pour in the Madeira. Reduce by half, then place the lettuce on top of the vegetables. Add the stock, bring to the boil, cover and braise until tender. This should take about 4–7 minutes, depending on the size of the lettuces. When ready, leave to cool in the liquid.

Joint the chicken and serve in bowls surrounded by the lovely braising liquid, some of the sautéed vegetables and the braised lettuce.

CABBAGES

We tend to treat cabbage as a bit of a poor relation. Too often it is over-boiled and memories of this have put many of us off it for years!

There are so many different varieties – red, white, Savoy, Spring, January King – available at different times of the year – all with their own particular qualities. And they're all great for different things. Red cabbage is best for stewing and pickling; white remains nice and firm, so works well for slaws and salads, as well as keeping its shape when steamed; early green cabbage, like Spring or January King, is great for braising and simply stewing in some butter and just a little water – its own excess water evaporates away, and it will cook in its own juices. It will be so, so sweet.

To get the best out of any cabbage, the real trick is either to cook it long and slow or super-fast. And don't forget – you can shred it raw and add a light mayonnaise or oil-based dressing to make a delicious coleslaw.

Here I have included two of my favourite slow methods to make the most of autumn and winter cabbage, when, let's face it, we all prefer those rich, warming dishes.

WHAT TO LOOK FOR:
- tight, compact vegetables, with no wilted leaves and a stalk that looks fresh.
- any cabbage should feel heavy for its size.

BRAISED WHITE CABBAGE & PORK CHOP

Serves 4

It wasn't until I worked for Marco Pierre White at The Criterion that I realised cabbage and pig make for a classic combination. Here we are braising the cabbage in wine and serving it with pork chop – a cut that doesn't always get the treatment it deserves, just like the cabbage. So let's allow them both a starring role.

5 tablespoons
vegetable oil
1 shallot, finely sliced
1 garlic clove,
   finely chopped
1 large white cabbage,
   quartered, cored, then
   finely shredded
100ml white wine
300ml chicken stock
sprig of thyme
2 bay leaves
4 pork chops
salt and freshly ground
   black pepper

Preheat the oven to 160°C/gas mark 3.

Place a large, lidded, heavy-based ovenproof casserole over a low to medium heat. Add 2 tablespoons of the vegetable oil, the shallot and garlic and cook until soft. Add the cabbage and sweat until most of its natural water content has evaporated. Pour in the wine, followed by the chicken stock, and bring it to the boil. Then add the thyme and bay leaves. Cover and place in the oven for 30 minutes, or until tender.

Season the pork chops on both sides with salt and pepper. Then place a heavy-based ovenproof frying pan over a medium heat. When hot, add the remaining vegetable oil then put the chops into the pan and colour on both sides. Transfer the pan to the oven for 10–12 minutes or until the pork juices run clear.

Serve the chops and the braised cabbage with some of the Apple Sauce on page 172.

RED CABBAGE & CONFIT DUCK LEG

Serves 4

Fatty, crispy, salt-rich duck shows off the sweet, spiced purpleness of the cabbage to perfection. And I think, with duck meat that falls off the bone like this, you want a vegetable that you can fork up with it just as easily. I like to serve this with a few sautéed potatoes on the side. You will need to start this recipe 24 hours before you want to serve it.

for the spice bag:
1 cinnamon stick, broken
6 juniper berries, crushed
3 cloves
2 star anise

for the cabbage:
1 red cabbage,
    quartered, cored,
    then finely shredded
150g soft brown sugar
250ml red wine
250ml port
200g duck fat
1 onion, sliced
4 Braeburn apples, peeled,
    quartered and cut
    crossways into
    2mm slices
sprig of thyme
1 bay leaf
250g redcurrant jelly
salt and freshly ground
    black pepper

for the confit:
4 large duck legs
100g salt
1 kg duck fat
sprig of thyme
handful of watercress,
    to garnish (optional)

Toast the spices in a dry frying pan to release the flavours. Set aside to cool, then wrap in muslin. Put the cabbage, sugar and spice bag into a non-metallic container. Pour in the red wine and port, cover and place in the fridge overnight.

The following morning, strain the cabbage from the wine, reserving both separately.

Heat the duck fat in a large, heavy-based saucepan. Add the onion, apple and herbs and sweat them, without colouring, until they are soft. Add the cabbage and cook for a further 4–5 minutes. Then add the reserved wine. Bring to the boil, then reduce the heat and cook the cabbage until the liquid has evaporated. Remove the pan from the heat, add the redcurrant jelly, season with salt and pepper and let cool.

To confit the duck legs, cover them with the salt and leave for 2 hours. Then wipe off the salt, and set the duck legs aside. Preheat the oven to 120°C/gas mark ½. Heat the duck fat in an ovenproof casserole and add the thyme. Then put the duck legs into the fat, and transfer the casserole to the oven for 3 hours. Remove and set aside to allow the duck to cool in the fat.

When you are ready to serve, gently reheat the cabbage over a low heat.

Preheat the grill to medium. Carefully remove the duck legs from the fat and place them on a baking tray. Put them under the grill to heat through and to make the skin nice and crispy, about 3–5 minutes.

Serve the hot duck alongside the cabbage, garnished with the watercress, if using.

Bryn's Tips: You can (and should) reuse the duck fat. Pour it into a jar and seal it. It will keep in the fridge for a month or so. Use it to fry anything. Obviously, it will be a little more flavoured than usual, as it has had the duck in it. But just imagine using it for the Hash Browns on page 143, with maybe a little of the duck stirred through before frying.

CAULIFLOWER

I've always thought that cauliflower is really underappreciated. It shouldn't be. It's a very versatile vegetable with its beautiful crisp white centre and bright green leaves. Alas, it's another one of those that suffers from the old overcooked syndrome. Or it's drowned in white sauce – which can be delicious if done properly, but all too often it is sitting in a weeping pool of greasy water.

Try to seek out the different varieties of cauliflower too: I particularly like the Romanesco, with its spire-like green florets. Its flavour is slightly grassier than the white cauliflower, but what a beauty on the plate.

A warning: cauliflower is a surprisingly unforgiving vegetable – it shifts from under- to overcooked very quickly. But it deserves our attention and, with a little care, we can liberate it from the prison of cheese sauce to make it into something special.

WHAT TO LOOK FOR:
- firm, white florets and crisp jade-green leaves.
- avoid yellowing or 'spotty' cauliflowers, or wilting leaves.

CAULIFLOWER SOUP WITH PINE NUTS & RAISINS

Serves 4

Much as I love soups, I feel they have to have texture, otherwise they can be too one-dimensional. This is a classic French cauliflower soup with an added twist of sweet raisins and crunchy toasted pine nuts to add that all-important texture and bring it right up to date.

50g butter
1 onion, peeled
   and sliced
1 small cauliflower,
   stalk removed and
   florets finely chopped
800ml milk
300ml double cream
pinch of sugar
salt and freshly ground
   black pepper

to garnish:
20g pine nuts, toasted
20g raisins
sprig of coriander,
   finely chopped

Melt the butter in a large, heavy-based saucepan without allowing it to colour. Add the onion, season with salt and pepper, and sweat gently for 2–3 minutes without letting it colour either. Then add the cauliflower, followed by the milk. Bring to the boil, and cook until the cauliflower is nice and soft. Add the double cream and bring back to the boil. Remove from the heat immediately – we want to keep that cauliflower flavour – and whizz in a blender or food-processor until smooth. If you're using a food-processor, let the soup cool a little before you whizz it.

Pass the soup through a fine sieve into a clean saucepan, season with salt and a pinch of sugar, and reheat if necessary.

Serve the soup in warmed bowls, garnished with the pine nuts, raisins and coriander.

Bryn's Tip: When you are prepping the cauliflower, some of the tips of the florets can break or crumble off: keep them! Use them to crumble over the top of salads and soups to add texture and flavour. We call this cauliflower couscous in our kitchen!

CHARRED CAULIFLOWER & SMOKED EEL SALAD

Serves 4

Grilling or charring the cauliflower sets this dish apart. It gives it a wonderful texture and taste that offsets the richness of the smoked eel.

1 whole cauliflower,
  trimmed
50ml olive oil
250g smoked eel,
  thinly sliced
bunch of watercress,
  leaves only
4 tablespoons Mustard
  Dressing (see page 216)
salt and freshly ground
  black pepper

Cut the cauliflower into florets then cut them in half: you need a flat side to place on the griddle. Put the cauliflower in a bowl, season with salt and pepper, and drizzle on the olive oil, ensuring the cauliflower is thoroughly coated.

Preheat a ridged griddle pan until medium hot. Place the flat side of the cauliflower on the griddle and cook for 1–2 minutes, or until it has taken on a good colour and is nicely charred. Turn over and cook for a further minute on the other side, then switch off the heat.

To serve, place the warm cauliflower on a plate. Arrange the smoked eel on and around the cauliflower, so the warmth of the cauliflower brings out the flavour in the eel. Distribute the watercress around the cauliflower and eel, and drizzle with the grainy mustard dressing.

RADISHES

My dad always used to eat radishes straight from the earth. He'd just give them a wipe, dip them in salt, and they were good to go. That's how I grew up eating radishes – raw. I'd never seen them cooked until I went to work in France where, as the new boy, my very first job was dipping radishes in butter. All day! We were using the long French Breakfast radishes (though who has radishes for breakfast, I don't know!), dipped into a rich, seasoned herb butter and placed on a chilled plate – a sophisticated step up from my dad's wipe-salt-chomp approach, and a real customer favourite.

Radishes actually belong to the mustard family, hence their lovely peppery bite, and come in a range of shapes and colours from palest blush pink to almost inky black with a startling white centre.

There's a trick to cooking radishes: you need to go hot and fast. Cook them too slowly and their colour will bleed and you'll lose the lovely, vibrant red, which is so much of their appeal on the plate.

WHAT TO LOOK FOR:
• small, firm radishes with fresh-looking leaves: remember, you can cook the leaves too.
• avoid anything remotely spongy.

RADISHES & HERB MAYONNAISE

Serves 4

This is so, so simple, but keeps people coming back for more. Crisp, red radishes; creamy, herb-flecked mayonnaise; eating with fingers... a very sexy little dish.

2 bunches of radishes

for the herb mayonnaise:
bunch of flat-leaf parsley,
    leaves only
sprig of tarragon
2 free range egg yolks
2 teaspoons white
    wine vinegar
2 teaspoons Dijon mustard
350ml vegetable oil
lemon juice, to taste
salt and freshly ground
    black pepper

Remove and discard any dead or yellow leaves from the radishes. Then give them and their remaining leaves a good wash in ice-cold water – this helps to keep them nice and crisp. Drain well, and pat them dry with kitchen paper. Set aside.

Blanch the herbs in boiling, salted water for 30 seconds, then remove with a slotted spoon. Place them immediately into a blender or food-processor and whizz until smooth. You may need to add a splash of water to help the herbs blend. When they're done, pass the purée through a fine sieve into a clean bowl, and put in the fridge to cool.

Using a food-processor with a whisk attachment, whisk the egg yolks, vinegar and mustard together. With the machine still running, slowly start to add the vegetable oil to the mix until it combines into a glossy emulsion. Fold in the cold herb purée. Season with salt, pepper and lemon juice to taste.

Serve the radishes with the herb mayonnaise.

Bryn's Tip: Instead of mayonnaise, you could add the herbs to a pack of softened unsalted butter, which I used to do at the Hôtel Negresco in Nice. Add a teaspoon of smooth Dijon mustard and season with salt and pepper. Serve with the radishes.

RADISH & PARMESAN GNOCCHI

Serves 4

Here, again, the natural flavourings of the two main ingredients give this dish real panache. Pillows of salty Parmesan gnocchi and crisp peppery radishes make this a real vegetarian favourite at Odette's.

bunch of radishes
50ml vegetable oil

for the gnocchi:
1–2 handfuls of rock
    salt for lining the
    roasting tin
3 large Desirée or other
    floury potatoes,
    unpeeled (to make
    about 500g of mash)
3 free range egg yolks
120g '00' flour,
    plus extra for dusting
80g grated Parmesan
    cheese
1 teaspoon salt
50g butter
handful of freshly chopped
    flat-leaf parsley and
    chives, to finish
salt and freshly ground
    black pepper

Preheat the oven to 160°C/gas mark 3.

Line a roasting tin with a layer of rock salt, a maximum of 2cm thick. Place the potatoes on the salt (this helps to draw out their moisture) and bake in the oven until soft, approximately 1–1½ hours. When they are cooked, remove from the oven. Cut the potatoes in half carefully – watch out for the hot steam – then scoop out the warm potato into a large bowl and mash until smooth.

Add the egg yolks, flour, Parmesan and salt and mix well until everything comes together as a dough. It should feel silky and pliable – like putty. Divide the mixture equally into four pieces. Dust your hands and the work surface with extra flour, then roll each piece into a long sausage shape about 1cm in diameter. Cut each sausage into 2.5cm lengths, and place on a floured board or tray.

Bring a large pan of salted water to a rolling boil. Drop in the gnocchi – you can probably do half of them at once. As soon as they start to float back up to the surface, they are ready. Remove with a slotted spoon to a colander while you cook the remainder.

Prepare the radishes carefully, removing and reserving their leaves (discard any that are dead or yellow). Give the radishes and the leaves a good wash in ice-cold water – this helps to keep them nice and crisp. Drain well, and pat them dry with kitchen paper. Set the leaves aside for later.

Cut the radishes in half and season them with salt and pepper. Heat the oil in a large frying pan and add the radishes, cut-side down. Do not turn. And do not crowd the pan; cook in two batches if necessary. Cook for about 2–3 minutes, or until golden brown. Remove from the pan and set aside to keep warm.

Melt the butter in the frying pan used for the radishes. Add the cooked gnocchi, the radishes and their leaves. Mix well, then remove from the hob. The radish leaves will wilt in the heat of the gnocchi. Season with salt and pepper. To serve, place in a bowl and scatter with the fresh herbs.

Bryn's Tip: Smear a tablespoon of the Homemade Pesto on page 205 onto each plate and then place the gnocchi and radishes on top.

RADISH, SAMPHIRE & MARINATED SEA TROUT

Serves 6

Samphire's a real favourite. It tastes of the sea, so its saltiness makes it a perfect foil for radishes. With the clean zinginess of the sea trout, this is truly one of my favourite dishes. The citrus dressing will almost give the fish a mild cure, but since the trout is essentially raw, do make sure you buy the best quality fish you can.

zest and juice of 2 oranges
zest and juice of 2 lemons
zest and juice of 2 limes
2 tablespoons honey
150ml olive oil
100g samphire
1 side of wild sea trout
6 radishes, trimmed and
   sliced very thinly
handful of chervil, parsley
   and/or chives, leaves
   picked and torn
salt and freshly ground
   black pepper

First make a dressing by blending the orange, lemon and lime juice in a large bowl with the honey and a pinch of salt. Gradually add the olive oil, whisking gently, until it emulsifies. Set aside.

Blanch the samphire in plenty of boiling, salted water for 1 minute, and then plunge immediately into iced water to stop it from cooking further. Set aside.

Slice the sea trout as thinly as possibly, overlap the slices on a large plate or shallow dish, drizzle half of the dressing over the fish, cover and refrigerate for 20 minutes before serving.

Put the radishes in a bowl with the samphire and season with salt and pepper.

To serve, scatter the radishes and samphire over the sea trout. Drizzle the remaining dressing over the top and finish with the fresh herbs.

Bryn's Tip: You can replace the sea trout with salmon if you prefer.

SPROUTS

When you cook seasonally, you face a bit of a challenge if you don't like sprouts. Come the winter, they're about all that's out there!

I was not a fan as a kid – I don't think many of us were. Except my brother Gareth, but that's another story. But when I became a chef I realised that there was a lot that was good about this much-maligned brassica, and that it could be prepared and cooked in a wide variety of ways, from steaming to creaming to stir-frying.

The key thing with sprouts is to preserve their colour. If you keep the colour, you keep the flavour. We don't want to have to look at (or eat) grey, over-cooked mini cabbages. We want to keep their brightness, their greenness, to remind us of the vegetables to come as the days grow longer.

WHAT TO LOOK FOR:
• tightly packed leaves, a bright green colour and preferably still on their long stick.
• choose the smallest sprouts, which are the sweetest.

CREAMED SPROUTS & ROAST PHEASANT

Serves 4

This recipe came about when we had a glut of winter brassica in the kitchen. The cream gently coats the sprouts and adds depth and a richness that is set off with the salty bacon and the gamey bird.

2 medium pheasants, gutted and dressed for roasting
2 tablespoons olive oil
6 rashers streaky bacon
250g Brussels sprouts
50g butter
200ml double cream
salt and freshly ground black pepper

Preheat the oven to 180°C/gas mark 4.

Season the pheasant with salt and pepper. Heat a frying pan until hot then add the olive oil. Seal the pheasants until golden all over.

Transfer the birds to a roasting tin, lay the bacon over their breasts and put into the oven for 15–20 minutes, or until cooked. They should remain a little pink in the middle.

Remove from the oven, take off and reserve the bacon rashers, cover the birds with tin foil and set aside in a warm place to rest.

Slice the sprouts as thinly as possible. Melt the butter in a large saucepan without letting it colour. Add the sliced sprouts, season with salt and pepper, then cook them as quickly as possible without letting them colour. The water from the sprouts should be released in this cooking process. Once all the liquid has evaporated, add the double cream, bring back to the boil and simmer until the cream reduces and just coats the sprouts.

To serve, remove the meat from the pheasant. Serve with the sprouts and the lovely crispy bacon on the side.

SPROUTS & CHESTNUTS WITH ROASTED PARTRIDGE

Serves 4

This dish just screams autumn to me. The sprouts on their sticks are popping up everywhere, chestnuts are being roasted on street corners, and the season's game is in. I think this dish makes for a delightful, simple combination of flavours. Just remember: do not overcook those sprouts!

4 partridges, gutted and dressed for roasting
3 tablespoons vegetable oil
250g Brussels sprouts, trimmed
100g cooked chestnuts (sold vacuum-packed)
50g butter
sprig of thyme, leaves only
salt and freshly ground black pepper

Preheat the oven to 180°C/gas mark 4.

Season the partridges with salt and pepper. Heat a frying pan until hot then add 2 tablespoons of the oil. Seal the partridges until golden all over.

Transfer the birds to a roasting tin and put into the oven for 10–15 minutes, or until cooked. They should remain a little pink in the middle. Remove from the oven, cover with tin foil and set aside in a warm place to rest.

Drop the Brussels sprouts whole into boiling, salted water. When just cooked, but still firm and green, remove them from the heat and submerge in ice-cold water until cold. Drain and dry them thoroughly with kitchen paper.

Cut the sprouts and the chestnuts in half. Heat the remaining vegetable oil in a heavy-based frying pan and add the sprouts. Season with salt and pepper. Once the sprouts start taking some colour, add the chestnuts, then the butter and cook for a further 2–3 minutes. Finish off with the thyme leaves.

Serve the partridge with a bowl of sprouts and chestnuts on the side.

WATERCRESS

All too often, people use watercress as a garnish. With its freshness and its peppery bite, it deserves much more of a starring role too. After all, it's one of the oldest leaf vegetables consumed by man, known to be popular with the ancient Persians, who used it to aid their children's growth, and the Romans, who loved it in salads and thought it cleared the mind and helped with decision-making. And it's packed with vitamin C, which led Captain Cook to include it in his sailors' diets when he circumnavigated the world. I think it's a fantastic ingredient. It works well with fish, it adds punch to orange and fennel salad, and makes an excellent soup too. Watercress is at its best when it's as fresh as possible, so use it as soon as you can after buying it. But if you have to store it, keep it in a plastic bag in the fridge or submerged in cold water.

WHAT TO LOOK FOR:
- dark green leaves – the darker the better.

WATERCRESS SOUP & POACHED DUCK EGG

Serves 4

Technically, watercress is not a brassica. It's actually a nasturtium, one of the mustard family, Cruciferae, but I really wanted to include this recipe here. The pepperiness of watercress acts as a wonderful foil to the innate creaminess of the duck eggs. And the beauty of including the duck eggs is that they spill their yolk into the soup to thicken it. An all-round win win, I think.

for the poached eggs:
4 duck eggs
1 tablespoon vinegar
pinch of salt

for the soup:
100g butter
1 onion, peeled
  and sliced
1 large potato,
  peeled and sliced
1.2 litres good
  vegetable stock
500g watercress,
  washed and trimmed
sea salt and freshly
  ground black pepper

Crack the eggs into 4 teacups or small ramekins and prepare a bowl of iced water. Bring a medium saucepan of water to a rolling boil, and add the vinegar and the salt. One by one, carefully lower in the eggs. They will sink to the bottom of the pan, and, as they do, the white will come up and around the yolk. After about 30 seconds, the eggs will start rising up through the water again. At this point, scoop them out with a slotted spoon and put them immediately into the bowl of iced water to stop them cooking. When they are cold, remove from the water with the slotted spoon, and set aside to drain. When you are ready to use the eggs, reheat them in boiling water for 30 seconds.

Melt the butter in a large, heavy-based saucepan over a gentle heat without allowing it to colour. Add the onion and let it sweat gently for about 4–5 minutes or until the onion is soft. Add the potato and sweat for a further 1–2 minutes. Season with salt then add the stock and bring it to the boil. Simmer for 2–3 minutes, or until the potato is cooked, then add the watercress. Bring everything back to the boil, then remove from the heat and blend with an immersion blender or in a food-processor until it's nice and smooth. If you're using a food-processor, let the soup cool a little before you whizz it. Pass the soup through a fine sieve into a clean saucepan, and season with salt and pepper to taste.

To serve, place the warm duck egg in a bowl, season with salt and pepper, and pour the watercress soup around it. Try not to drown the egg with the soup, just surround it like an island.

COURGETTE SUPPER CLUB

Courgettes (or zucchini) are really just little marrows and at every stage of their growth they're beautiful to cook with. The flowers, delicate and summery, are divine dipped in tempura batter and deep-fried. Baby courgettes are delicious simply brushed with olive oil and roasted or grilled on the barbecue. And I love courgette chips – in fact, there's one place in London I head for specifically to order them. Try to hunt out different varieties other than the familiar green ones: the globe courgettes have a subtle sweetness, while yellow courgettes offer a firmer texture and a punchier flavour, as well as that glorious shock of Van Gogh yellow. And courgettes are super-easy to grow – I have friends who grows them on their roof terrace. Fresh and vibrant, they are a herald of summer. And they're one of my real favourite vegetables.

WHAT TO LOOK FOR:
- firm, glossy-skinned and not too large courgettes have the best flavour.

MARINATED COURGETTE, PINE NUT & PARMESAN SALAD

Serves 4

This salad idea was inspired by a holiday in Italy, before which I had never really thought about serving courgettes raw. Not only were they visually stunning, but also delicious with a fresh, crisp bite. Here they are simply dressed and served with crunchy toasted pine nuts and tangy Parmesan.

for the dressing:
50ml good balsamic
    vinegar
150ml good olive oil
squeeze of lemon juice
salt and freshly ground
    black pepper

for the salad:
3 yellow courgettes,
    trimmed
3 green courgettes,
    trimmed
80g pine nuts, toasted
3 bunches of wild
    rocket leaves
100g Parmesan cheese
    shavings
salt

To make the dressing, pour the balsamic vinegar into a large bowl and season with salt and pepper. Whisk in the olive oil and finish with a squeeze of lemon juice.

Slice all the courgettes lengthways using a mandolin – you want them about 3mm thick. Place the strips in a colander, season with a little salt and leave to stand for 7–8 minutes to extract all the excess water. When the courgettes are ready, set them aside on kitchen paper and pat dry thoroughly.

Arrange the courgettes on 4 large plates, evenly distributing the yellow and green ones, and, for best effect, try to create some height. Sprinkle with the toasted pine nuts and drizzle with some of the balsamic dressing. Add a layer of rocket leaves and drizzle them with the rest of the balsamic dressing.

Finish the dish with a scattering of Parmesan shavings.

COURGETTE FLOWERS & HALIBUT

Serves 4

So often the courgette's beautiful buttercup-yellow flowers are served battered and fried. I wanted a lighter approach and to really capture their flavour, so here they are steamed. Served with a ratatouille-style stuffing and lightly pan-fried halibut, this is a delightful lunch or supper dish, and a great part of this four-course courgette feast!

for the courgettes:
1 tablespoon
   vegetable oil
1 courgette, trimmed
   and cut into 1cm dice
sprig of thyme,
   leaves only
50g Spiced Tomato
   Chutney (see page 217)
4 courgette flowers,
   still attached to
   the courgette

for the halibut:
4 x 160g halibut fillets
1 tablespoon olive oil
50g butter
salt and freshly ground
   black pepper

Heat the vegetable oil in a saucepan over a medium heat. Add the diced courgette and the thyme leaves, season with salt and pepper and cook without colouring until the courgette is soft and all the liquid has evaporated. Remove from the heat and add just enough tomato chutney to bind the mixture together – it must not be too wet. Set aside to cool.

Carefully open the courgette flowers without breaking them or snapping them off from the courgette. Check the insides of the flowers are clean, and then stuff them with the cooled courgette mixture. Close over the flower tops to enclose the mixture, then carefully wrap each flower in clingfilm to protect it from moisture during cooking. Put the courgettes in the fridge until you're ready to cook.

Transfer the courgettes to a steamer and cook for 5–6 minutes or until the courgette is cooked. Unwrap the flowers and set aside to keep warm.

Season the halibut with salt and pepper. Heat a large heavy-based frying pan over a medium heat. Add the olive oil. When it's hot, put in the halibut and cook for 2–3 minutes. Add the butter and let it melt and foam up. Then turn over the halibut and cook for a further 1–2 minutes on the other side.

Serve the fish alongside the stuffed courgette flowers.

DEEP-FRIED COURGETTE WITH PORK CUTLET & TOMATO & OLIVE SAUCE

Serves 2

Courgettes and tomatoes: come on! You know what I mean! If you have courgettes growing in your garden, I am pretty sure you have tomatoes somewhere too. They're such a natural pairing. And a chunky pork cutlet is terrific for absorbing all those sunny flavours.

for the courgettes:
2 courgettes, trimmed
   and cut to the size of
   thin chips
150g plain flour
salt and freshly ground
   black pepper

for the pork:
1 large pork cutlet with
   2 bones in (2 chops
   joined together)
1 tablespoon olive oil
50g butter

*for the tomato and
olive sauce:*
4 plum tomatoes
50ml olive oil
1 tablespoon
   chopped shallot
½ garlic clove, chopped
1 tablespoon Spiced
   Tomato Chutney
   (see page 217)
4 green olives
4 basil leaves, torn
salt and freshly ground
   black pepper

Preheat the oven to 160°C/gas mark 3.

Put the courgettes in a colander placed over a bowl and season with salt. Mix well and leave to stand for 30 minutes. When ready, transfer the courgettes to kitchen paper to dry thoroughly.

Season the pork with salt and pepper. Heat the olive oil and half the butter in a large casserole over a medium heat and brown the pork all over until golden and caramelised. Transfer to the oven for 20 minutes or until the juices run clear. Remove from the oven, cover and leave to rest for 10–15 minutes.

Preheat your deep-fat fryer to 180°C.

Put the flour into a large bowl, season with salt and pepper. Toss the courgettes thoroughly in the seasoned flour. Then deep-fry for 2–3 minutes or until golden. Remove and set aside on kitchen paper to drain.

To make the sauce, blanch the tomatoes in boiling, salted water for 10 seconds, then put them into ice-cold water. When they're cold, peel off the skins, cut them in half, then scoop out and discard the seeds. Cut the tomato flesh into 5mm dice. Set aside.

Put the olive oil, shallot, garlic and tomato chutney in a small saucepan and heat gently – do not allow it to boil. Add the olives, diced tomatoes and basil, and season with salt and pepper. Set aside and keep warm.

To serve, cut the pork cutlet in half. Divide the tomato sauce between 2 plates, place the pork on top and serve the fried courgettes on the side.

COURGETTE & LEMON THYME CAKE

Serves 8–10

Courgette is such a moist vegetable it lends that same quality to this cake. This is light, lemony and delicious served either as a dessert or with a cup of tea.

125ml vegetable oil,
plus extra for greasing
3 free range eggs
150g caster sugar
250g plain flour
1 teaspoon bicarbonate
of soda
1 teaspoon baking
powder
3 large courgettes,
green or yellow,
trimmed and
finely grated
sprig of lemon thyme,
leaves only

Preheat the oven to 180°C/gas mark 4. Grease and line a 450g loaf tin.

Put the oil, eggs and sugar into a large bowl and beat until creamy. Sift in the flour, bicarbonate of soda and baking powder and continue to beat until combined. Stir in the grated courgette and add the thyme leaves.

Pour the mixture into the prepared tin and bake for 25–30 minutes. Remove from the oven and leave the cake to cool in the tin for about 5 minutes. Turn out and cool completely on a wire rack.

This goes really well with the Lemon Curd on page 190.

CUCUMBERS

This is another vegetable that is often found shrivelling in the back of the fridge. Poor old cucumber, it's almost always served cold, raw and chopped, which is such a shame because it has a beautiful and subtle flavour. When I worked at The Criterion for Marco Pierre White, we used to make his signature dish: warm cucumber with oysters. We'd gently warm the oyster juices with diced cucumber and serve the oysters on the half shell with this mixture on top. Simple and stunning. And it made me realise that there's more to cucumber than a sandwich! They are wonderful pickled, braised, sliced raw or grated, in soups (see below) and charred or grilled (see opposite).

Cucumbers are at their best when they are young and firm: store them in the fridge and use them quickly.

WHAT TO LOOK FOR:
* firm, bright green and smooth skin with no sponginess.

CHILLED CUCUMBER SOUP

Serves 4

Cold, pale green and refreshing, this soup is wonderful as a starter or a light lunch. You could flake some smoked fish into the soup, or poach a few oysters and float them on top, for a contrast of textures and flavours. You will need to start this soup the day before you need it.

6 cucumbers, deseeded and cut into 3cm dice
bunch of chervil
bunch of tarragon
bunch of chives
juice of 1 lemon
300ml double cream
250g mascarpone
2 tablespoons creamed horseradish
olive oil
salt and freshly ground black pepper

Put the cucumber into a large bowl. Strip the leaves from the chervil and tarragon, reserving a few whole leaves for the garnish, and roughly tear them into the bowl, along with the chives. Add the lemon juice and season with salt and pepper. Mix well, cover the bowl and place in the fridge overnight.

The following day, transfer the contents of the bowl to a blender or food-processor and whizz until smooth, then pass through a fine sieve into a clean bowl, pressing through as much of the liquid as you can. Add the cream, mascarpone and horseradish to the cucumber liquid, and mix well. Season with salt and pepper.

To serve, pour into bowls and garnish with the reserved chervil and tarragon leaves and a drizzle of olive oil.

CHARRED CUCUMBER, SQUID & CHILLI

Serves 4

Charring cucumber is a little unusual, but you will see how much this method brings out the 'cucumberiness'. The textural contrast of soft squid and slightly crisp cucumber punched through with chilli makes this a perfect starter or light lunch on a summer's day.

1 medium squid,
  cleaned
1 red chilli,
  finely chopped
juice and zest of 1 lime
pinch of sugar
1 garlic clove, crushed
4 tablespoons vegetable
  oil, plus extra for drizzling
2 cucumbers, peeled and
  sliced into 1cm rounds
2 spring onions, trimmed
  and chopped
salt and freshly ground
  black pepper

Cut the squid into bite-sized pieces, and put into a bowl. Add the chilli, lime juice and zest, sugar, garlic, sea salt, pepper and 3 tablespoons of the vegetable oil. Cover the bowl and set aside in the fridge to marinate for 1 hour.

Put the cucumber slices in a colander placed over a bowl and season with sea salt. Leave to stand for 30 minutes, then transfer the slices to kitchen paper to blot up the excess water. Ensure they are nice and dry.

Heat a griddle pan until very hot. Drizzle a little vegetable oil over the cucumber slices and cook them, in batches if necessary, on the griddle for 2 minutes until nicely charred. Then turn them over and turn off the heat.

Remove the squid from the bowl, reserving the marinade. Heat a large sauté pan over a medium heat. Add the remaining tablespoon of oil and, when it starts to smoke, add the squid. Cook for 30 seconds before you stir or toss it with a wooden spoon. Then add the marinade to the pan, and cook for a further 30 seconds. Finally, add the spring onions and lightly stir through.

To serve, place the warm cucumber into bowls. Season with sea salt, then pour over the cooked squid and the marinade.

PUMPKIN & SQUASH SUPPER CLUB

These versatile and hardy vegetables are not just for Hallowe'en, you know! They come in a multitude of varieties that are deserving of our attention. In general, pumpkins and squash hold a lot of water. So, in cooking them, we're looking to remove that water in order to concentrate their natural flavours. That said, the water content varies significantly between varieties.

Once you feel confident with the squash used in the recipes here, you can experiment with other types. At home, I like to do just this: stuffing Munchkins as a side dish or sautéing slices of Turban or Butternut squash. Small Acorn squash are lovely baked whole. In the restaurant, though, I tend to stick with Butternuts. They're very consistent in their texture; they behave themselves impeccably! However, for the Pumpkin Pie I advocate a winter squash, the green-skinned Kabocha, a Japanese variety that's readily available from most supermarkets in the West. It has intensely coloured flesh and an exceptional natural sweetness, making it perfect for desserts.

WHAT TO LOOK FOR:
- firmness and a heaviness for their size.
- if you are buying a wedge or slice of pumpkin ensure the flesh has a nice close texture – no stringiness.

BUTTERNUT SQUASH & PARMESAN SOUP

Serves 4

This soup has that salty-sweet flavour that most people love, as well as being beautiful to look at. Serve on a cold day with crusty rolls or slices of the fresh Shallot Bread on page 33.

---

for the soup:
800ml good
    vegetable stock
50g butter
1 onion, peeled
    and chopped
1kg Butternut squash,
    peeled, deseeded
    and cubed (reserve
    20g for the garnish)
100g Parmesan cheese,
    plus its outside
    rind, chopped
salt and freshly
    ground black pepper

for the garnish:
20g Butternut squash
    seeds, taken from
    the squash
2 tablespoons vegetable
    oil, or enough to cover
    the seeds
100g fresh cep or porcini
    mushrooms, cut into
    bite-sized pieces
bunch of chives, chopped
1 tablespoon
    unsalted butter
20g Parmesan cheese,
    cut into 5mm dice

First, make the soup. Pour the stock into a heavy-based saucepan and bring to the boil over a medium heat.

Melt the butter in a large saucepan over a low heat, add the onion and cook without allowing it to colour. When it's soft, add the diced Butternut squash and sweat over a medium heat for 2 minutes. Add the boiling vegetable stock, bring back to the boil, then add the Parmesan. Simmer for 10 minutes, or until the squash is cooked, and season with salt and pepper to taste. Transfer to a food-processor or blender and whizz until smooth. Pass through a fine sieve back into the cleaned saucepan. Set aside.

To make the garnish, toast the Butternut squash seeds in a dry frying pan over a low heat until fragrant, then cover with the vegetable oil and simmer gently for 5 minutes. Remove from the oil with a slotted spoon and set aside to drain on kitchen paper, reserving the oil.

Heat a frying pan, add a little of the Butternut-seed infused oil then add the ceps or porcini. Season with salt and pepper, and cook until golden all over. Then add the chives. Scoop out the mushrooms and set aside to keep warm.

Heat the butter in another frying pan, and gently sweat the diced pumpkin for a couple of minutes, until just cooked through. Remove with a slotted spoon and set aside on kitchen paper to drain.

To serve, bring the soup to the boil, and pour it into bowls. Sprinkle with the diced Parmesan and pumpkin, then add the diced ceps. Finish with the squash seeds and a little of the oil used to simmer them.

Bryn's Tip: Don't discard the hard rind from a wedge of Parmesan. Pop it into a plastic bag and store in the freezer: it adds a wonderful depth of flavour to soups and stews.

BUTTERNUT SQUASH PIZZA WITH SEARED SCALLOPS & BLUE CHEESE

Serves 6

You may think pumpkin, scallops and a scattering of blue cheese make unusual companions, but the subtle, creamy brininess of scallops, the butteriness of squash and the tang of blue cheese make this tartine-like pizza an absolute winner.

for the dough:
5g fresh yeast
175ml lukewarm water
250g strong white
   bread flour, plus
   extra for dusting
1 teaspoon salt
50ml olive oil

for the topping:
1 small Butternut
   squash, peeled
sprig of rosemary, leaves
   only, roughly chopped
olive oil, for drizzling
1 tablespoon
   vegetable oil
4 large scallops, each cut
   into 2 discs (no roe)
squeeze of lemon juice
100g blue cheese,
   crumbled
bunch of rocket
salt and freshly ground
   black pepper

Grease and line a 40 x 30cm baking tray. Dissolve the yeast in the lukewarm water. Put the flour, salt and olive oil into a large bowl and pour in the yeasty water. Using your hands, mix the flour and water together until you have a cohesive mass, and everything holds together well – it should not be claggy!

Turn out the dough onto a floured surface and knead for about 5 minutes until it's nice and stretchy and has a silky feel.

Roll out the dough to the size of the baking tray, then place on the tray and transfer to the fridge to rest for about 2 hours.

Cut the squash in half lengthways. Discard the seeds, and then cut the flesh into thin slices. Set aside.

Preheat the oven to 180°C/gas mark 4. Remove the tray from the fridge. Arrange the sliced squash over the dough. Season with salt, pepper and the chopped rosemary, then drizzle with olive oil. Leave the pizza to stand for 30 minutes to return to room temperature and for the dough to prove slightly.

Transfer the tray to the oven for 25–35 minutes or until the pizza is cooked, risen and golden. Remove from the oven and leave to cool for 5 minutes.

Heat a heavy-based frying pan until very hot. Add the vegetable oil. Put the scallops in the hot pan and cook for 1 minute on one side, then turn over and cook for 30 seconds on the other – you want them slightly under-cooked in the centre. Remove from the pan and season with salt and a squeeze of lemon.

To serve, place the scallops over the Butternut squash, sprinkle with the blue cheese and finish with a scattering of rocket leaves.

BUTTERNUT RISOTTO & SAGE BUTTER

Serves 4
as a starter

At the Supper Club we serve this with Slow-roasted Pork Belly (page 48) as the textures and flavours marry so well. But the risotto is a perfect stand alone as a meat-free starter, light lunch or supper. If you serve it with the pork belly, you need to start the day before you want to eat it.

for the risotto:
1 small Butternut squash,
    peeled
sprig of thyme,
    leaves only
50ml olive oil
1 litre good vegetable
    stock
50g butter
2 shallots, peeled and
    finely chopped
150g risotto rice
100ml white wine
50g Parmesan cheese,
    finely grated
salt and freshly ground
    black pepper

for the sage butter:
50g butter
juice of ½ lemon
1–2 tablespoons chopped
    sage leaves

Preheat the oven to 180°C/gas mark 4.

Cut the squash in half lengthways and scoop out the seeds. Season the flesh with salt and pepper, sprinkle with the thyme leaves and drizzle with olive oil. Wrap it in tin foil and put in the oven for 40 minutes or until soft.

When it's ready, remove the squash from the oven and leave until it is cool enough to handle. Using a dessertspoon, carefully remove the squash flesh from the skin and set aside. Try to keep some nice whole pieces, but don't worry if you have a lot of broken bits as this will add good texture to the risotto.

Pour the stock into a saucepan and bring to the boil over a medium heat. Reduce to a simmer and keep the pan within easy reach until needed.

Heat the butter in a large, heavy-based saucepan. Add the chopped shallot and cook for 2–3 minutes or until soft. Add the rice, stir well to coat it nicely with the butter and shallots and cook for 1 minute. Pour in the white wine and stir continuously until it has all been absorbed. Add a ladleful of the simmering stock to the rice, stirring all the time, and cook until the stock has been absorbed before adding another ladle. Repeat the process until the rice is tender but retains a little bite – this should take about 20 minutes.

When the risotto is ready, remove the pan from the heat and stir in the Parmesan. Cover the pan to allow it to melt. Add the Butternut squash, stirring in gently. If the risotto feels a little too firm, stir through a little more stock before serving. Cover the pan and set aside to keep warm.

To make the sage butter, melt the butter in a heavy-based frying pan over a medium heat until it is liquid and golden. Remove the pan from the heat, stand back and squeeze in the lemon juice. Then add the sage leaves.

To serve, put the risotto into a bowl and pour over the sage butter. Serve with slices of the Pork Belly on page 48.

PUMPKIN PIE

Serves 8

A North American Thanksgiving classic – and fast becoming a firm favourite in my kitchen too.

1 quantity of Sweet Pastry
(see page 219)
flour, for dusting
350g Kabocha squash,
diced
1 free range egg
5 free range egg yolks
½ vanilla pod,
seeds only
175g caster sugar
200ml double cream

Preheat the oven to 180°C/gas mark 4. Lightly grease a 23cm tart tin with a removable base.

Roll out the pastry on a lightly floured surface and use it to carefully line the tart tin. Lay a sheet of greaseproof paper over the pastry, weigh it down with baking beans and bake blind in the oven for 15–20 minutes. Remove from the oven, lift out the paper and beans and set the tart shell aside to cool.

Put the diced squash into a heavy-based saucepan. Pour in enough water to come half way up the squash, cover the pan with a lid and bring up to the boil. Cook for 7–8 minutes. Remove the lid and stir the squash – if it isn't soft yet, continue to cook, uncovered, until it is. Remove from the heat and strain the squash through a colander, reserving the cooking liquor.

Put the squash into a blender or food-processor and whizz, adding just enough of the cooking liquor to help it along. You need the purée to be nice and thick. When ready, set aside to cool and then place in the fridge until cold.

Preheat the oven to 140°C/gas mark 1.

When the purée is cold, put it into a large bowl and add all the remaining ingredients. Mix together until well combined.

Pour the mixture into the tart case and place in the oven for 40 minutes or until golden and risen.

BROAD BEANS

My granddad used to grow broad beans. I have very happy memories of podding them in front of my favourite shows on the telly. But, as a kid, I never really liked them. At the time, we all tended to cook them in their skins, and I always thought they were a bit rubbery (sorry, mum). When I came to work in kitchens in London, I must have spent hours podding them, blanching them, and slipping off their grey skins to reveal that beautiful green jewel within. What a revelation! It was a key lesson: if ever there was something I didn't like when I was young, it always turned out that there was a secret to making it delicious!

WHAT TO LOOK FOR:
- broad beans are at their best when they are young, fresh-looking pods.
- try to pick the firmest pods with the least brown spots, and no pockets of air – those are the ones that tend to be a bit flabby and old.

BROAD BEANS, TARRAGON & POACHED CHICKEN

Serves 4

This is a lovely, simple dish, perfect for lunch or a light supper. Chicken and tarragon are a classic combination, and the beans give them extra colour, brightness and texture.

650ml good chicken stock
1 tablespoon olive oil
1 small onion, peeled
  and finely chopped
1 garlic clove, peeled
  and finely chopped
100g pearl barley
4 skinless chicken breasts
200g broad beans,
  shelled
sprig of tarragon,
  leaves only
salt and freshly ground
  black pepper

Pour the chicken stock into a large saucepan and bring to a simmer.

Meanwhile, heat the olive oil in another large saucepan over a medium heat and sweat the onion and garlic without allowing them to colour. When soft, add the pearl barley, season with salt and pepper, then pour in the hot stock. Bring to a simmer and cook for 30 minutes, or until the pearl barley is tender.

Season the chicken breasts with salt and pepper, then place them in the saucepan with the pearl barley, ensuring that they are submerged (you may need to add a little more stock or water). Poach for 12–14 minutes or until cooked. Then add the broad beans and cook for a further few minutes.

Serve in a large bowl sprinkled with the tarragon leaves.

Bryn's Tip: When you have lovely fresh, young beans, don't discard the pods. Just scrape them out gently, removing any of that white fur inside them. Then dip them in a light batter and deep-fry until crisp. Sprinkle with sea salt and serve as a snack.

BROAD BEAN & CHORIZO RISOTTO

Serves 4
as a starter

The lovely earthy-sweetness of fresh broad beans sits very comfortably next to the spicy chorizo in this simple and tasty risotto.

1 litre mushroom stock
  or good chicken stock,
  or a mix of both
1 tablespoon olive oil
50g cooking chorizo,
  chopped
50g butter
2 shallots, peeled
  and finely chopped
200g risotto rice
100ml white wine
100g broad beans,
  shelled
50g Parmesan cheese,
  grated
salt and freshly ground
  black pepper

Pour the stock into a saucepan and bring to the boil over a medium heat. Reduce to a simmer and keep the pan within easy reach until needed.

Heat the olive oil in a heavy-based saucepan over a medium heat and cook the chorizo for 2–3 minutes. We don't want it to take on any colour at this point. Remove the chorizo from the pan with a slotted spoon, and set aside to drain.

Add the butter and shallots to the pan and cook until soft. Add the rice, stir well to coat it nicely with the butter and shallots and cook for 1 minute. Pour in the white wine and stir continuously until it has all been absorbed. Add a ladleful of the simmering stock to the rice, stirring all the time, and cook until the stock has been absorbed before adding another ladle. Repeat the process until the rice is tender but retains a little bite – this should take about 20 minutes.

Remove the pan from the heat and leave to rest, covered, for a few minutes.

Finally, stir the broad beans and Parmesan into the risotto. Then add the chorizo and stir it in gently.

If the risotto is too firm, add a little stock before serving.

PEA SUPPER CLUB

Peas always remind me of my granddad. I used to sit with him in his walled garden, podding what we'd just picked for Sunday lunch. The trouble was that we'd eat them – peas do that to you – so we'd get back to my mum, preparing lunch for ten, with only enough peas for four. She'd go mental!

When you squeeze a freshly podded pea, a white liquid should exude, which is the natural starch and sugar. It's a sure sign of freshness – something peas lose very quickly, and which is retained by the freezing process. Most frozen peas are under ice inside two hours. They're a fantastic product, second only to the ones you pick yourself, and a lot of chefs use them. Their only drawback is that, once thawed, they still look like frozen peas, so I tend to use them only in purées and soups.

You can use a lot of the pea plant. The shoots freshen a green salad, the peas themselves can be used in a whole host of ways, and the pods, which also have a glorious natural sweetness, make a delicious stock that can often be a great base for a vegetable soup. All of which made the pea the perfect choice for this Supper Club project.

WHAT TO LOOK FOR:
- young, firm, fresh, bright-green pods – a good indication of the sweetest peas.
- avoid any that feel a bit hollow.

PEA SOUP

Serves 4

Enriched with a little double cream and with a hint of mint, this is a pea soup for all seasons. The secret is to cook the peas in pea stock.

---

1 litre Pea Stock
  (see page 218)
100g butter
1 onion, peeled
  and sliced
1kg peas (frozen are fine)
125ml double cream
3 sprigs of mint,
  leaves only
salt and freshly ground
  black pepper

Bring the stock to the boil in a large saucepan.

Melt the butter in a second large saucepan over a medium heat. Cook the onion in the butter until it's soft but hasn't taken any colour. Add the peas, mix well, and cook for 3–4 minutes. Then pour on the boiling stock. Bring back to the boil and cook the peas until soft. Add the double cream. Remove from the heat and carefully blitz in a blender or food-processor along with the mint leaves. Pass through a fine sieve into a clean saucepan. Season with salt and pepper to taste.

Serve hot or cold.

PEA & BACON SALAD

Serves 4

When I was growing up, my dad had a signature dish: peas and bacon in a pea stock thickened with flour. It was delicious. I still love that combination of sweet peas and salty bacon. This salad is simple and light and can be enjoyed all year round.

2 tablespoons
 vegetable oil
200g bacon lardons
1 shallot, peeled
 and finely chopped
100ml Odette's House
 Dressing (see page 217)
400g cooked peas
 (frozen are fine)
2 tablespoons
 marjoram leaves
100g pea shoots
salt and freshly ground
 black pepper

Place a frying pan over a medium heat. Add the vegetable oil and cook the bacon until golden brown. Reduce the heat, add the shallot and cook for 2 minutes. When the bacon and shallots are cooked, remove the pan from the heat, pour in the dressing and set aside to cool for 3–4 minutes.

When it's cooled, add the peas and the marjoram to the frying pan. Season with salt and pepper then transfer the bacon and pea mixture to a large serving bowl and set aside until completely cold.

Mix in the pea shoots and serve.

Bryn's Tips: When pea shoots are not in season, use some watercress or mixed leaves.

You could serve this with poached or grilled salmon supremes to make a more substantial dish.

PEA RISOTTO & LAMB FILLET

Serves 4

Salty Parmesan, sweet peas and creamy risotto, topped off with perfectly cooked but still juicily pink lamb.

Without the lamb, this dish makes a wonderful starter.

---

for the lamb:
8 x 100g lamb fillets
1 tablespoon
    vegetable oil
salt and freshly ground
    black pepper

for the risotto:
1 litre Pea Stock
    (see page 218)
50g butter
2 shallots, finely chopped
200g risotto rice
100ml white wine
50g Parmesan cheese,
    grated
200g peas, fresh or frozen
small bunch of mint,
    leaves only, chopped

Season the lamb fillets with salt and pepper. Heat the vegetable oil in a frying pan until hot.

Pop in the fillets and cook for 2–3 minutes on each side until nicely brown but still pink inside. Remove from the pan and set aside to rest, covered with foil.

Pour the stock into a saucepan and bring to the boil over a medium heat. Reduce to a simmer and keep the pan within easy reach until needed.

Heat the butter in a heavy-based saucepan over a medium heat. Add the shallots to the pan and cook until soft. Add the rice, stir well to coat it nicely with the butter and shallots and cook for 1 minute. Pour in the white wine and stir continuously until it has all been absorbed. Add a ladleful of the simmering stock to the rice, stirring all the time, and cook until the stock has been absorbed before adding another ladle. Repeat the process until the rice is tender but retains a little bite – this should take about 20 minutes.

Remove the pan from the heat and leave to rest, covered, for a few minutes.

Stir the Parmesan and the peas into the risotto. If the risotto feels a little too firm, stir through a little stock before serving.

Add the mint and stir through gently.

Serve 2 lamb fillets per person, sliced and placed alongside the risotto.

PEA BAVAROIS

Serves 6

A dessert made with peas just makes sense – cool, green, sweet little morsels puréed and whipped into a sexy, creamy custard. Mushy peas never tasted so good! You will need to start this dessert the day before you want to serve it.

250g peas
20g caster sugar
water, to cover
10g leaf gelatine
2 free range eggs,
    separated
50g caster sugar
200ml milk
300ml whipping cream

First make the purée. Put the peas and sugar into a saucepan and just cover with water. Then place the pan over a high heat and bring to the boil for 4–5 minutes, until the peas are just cooked. You may need to add more water as you cook the peas.

When the peas are cooked, strain them through a colander, reserving the cooking liquor, and put them into a blender or food-processor. Start to blend the peas, adding a little cooking liquor at a time, until smooth. Then pass through a fine sieve into a clean bowl. Leave it to cool, cover and keep the purée in the fridge until needed.

Soak the leaf gelatine in a little cold water.

Whisk together the egg yolks and sugar in a large bowl until thick and creamy.

Pour the milk into a heavy-based saucepan and bring to the boil. Remove from the heat and pour the hot milk onto the yolk mixture, whisking continuously. Pour the mixture back into the pan and cook over a low heat, stirring continuously with a wooden spoon, until the custard thickens and coats the back of the spoon. Remove from the heat. Add the strained gelatine and stir until it dissolves. Then pass the custard through a fine sieve into a clean bowl, cover, and set aside to cool.

When the mixture is completely cold, add the chilled pea purée and mix well. Set aside.

Whisk the cream in a large bowl until it makes soft peaks. Then, in a separate bowl, whisk the egg whites into soft peaks.

Gently fold the cream into the pea custard, followed by the egg whites, until the mixture is smooth and light. Pour the mixture into 6 ramekins and place in the fridge to set overnight.

When ready to serve, turn out onto individual plates.

RUNNER BEANS

The season for runner beans is so short that, to be honest, I don't want to mess them about too much. They're so perfect, just as they are. They're also easy to grow – they pretty much take care of themselves. Even if you only have a little outside space, it's worth putting up a little bamboo teepee for them to climb; you can only benefit – they'll be so super-fresh they'll taste of summer.

When cooking runner beans, you need to pay attention to their texture. There's a very fine line between their being under- and overdone. Underdone, they squeak when you bite them; overdone, they turn a little grey. So keep your eye on them, just as you would when you're cooking a steak, to ensure that they reach their perfect done-ness.

WHAT TO LOOK FOR:
- crisp, firm, young beans.

RUNNER BEANS, HAZELNUTS & HALIBUT

Serves 4

Hazelnuts and runner beans are very good together, and the natural oil of the nuts goes beautifully with fish, so this combination is just about perfect. The halibut is firm, yet pearlescently flaky. The beans are cooked until just crisp and the nuts give great crunch. The rich, silky oils bring the dish together, giving the whole thing a sheen – a luxurious finish without using butter.

4 x 160g halibut fillets
2 tablespoons
   vegetable oil
300g runner beans,
   trimmed and finely
   shredded lengthways
300ml good
   vegetable stock
50g butter
zest and juice of 1 lemon
20g hazelnuts, toasted
   and chopped in half
50ml hazelnut oil
salt and freshly ground
   black pepper

Season the halibut with salt and pepper. Heat the vegetable oil in a large frying pan over a medium hob. Pan-fry the fish for 3–4 minutes, then turn over and cook on the other side for a further 2 minutes or until the fish is done.

Put the runner beans in a medium saucepan. Pour in the vegetable stock, add the butter and season with salt and pepper. Place the pan over a high heat, bring to the boil and cook for 1–2 minutes until the butter and stock have come together and the runner beans are cooked. When ready, remove from the heat, add the lemon zest and juice and the hazelnuts. Set aside to keep warm.

To serve, pile the beans and hazelnuts onto warm plates, top with the halibut and drizzle over the hazelnut oil.

RUNNER BEANS, WILD MUSHROOM & LAMB'S TONGUE SALAD

Serves 4

Wild mushrooms and runner beans have a real affinity, perhaps because they grow at virtually the same time. One is just ending as the other's season begins. The firm bite of the runner bean against the melting boskiness of the girolle, the crisply fried tongue and the sharp dressing... what's not to love about this earthy plate of food?

8 lambs' tongues
1 small onion, peeled and diced
1 small carrot, peeled and diced
sprig of thyme
300g runner beans, trimmed and finely shredded lengthways
50g butter
100g girolle mushrooms, cleaned
100ml Red Wine Dressing (see page 216)
50ml vegetable oil
salt and freshly ground black pepper

Wash the lambs' tongues in cold water. Put them into a large saucepan, add the onion, carrot and thyme and cover with water. Bring to a slow simmer over a low heat and cook for 2 hours, or until tender. You might need to top up the pan with more cold water.

When ready, remove the tongues from the liquid and, while they're still warm, peel off the skin and gristle with a small knife. Set aside to cool before transferring to the fridge to become completely cold. When cold, cut each tongue in half lengthways. Set aside.

Drop the runner beans into a saucepan of boiling, salted water and cook for 30 seconds. Then plunge immediately into ice-cold water to stop the cooking and to keep their colour. When cold, remove from the water and drain thoroughly in a colander. Set aside.

Melt the butter in a heavy-based frying pan over a medium heat. When it is foaming, add the girolles and cook until they have gained a little colour. Don't shake the pan – if you do, too much water will be released from the mushrooms and make the dish soggy. When they are ready, add the runner beans. Season with salt and pepper, pour in the dressing and remove from the heat. Set aside and keep warm.

Heat another frying pan over a medium heat, and add the vegetable oil. Crisp up the lambs' tongues in the pan until golden on all sides.

To serve, use a slotted spoon to scatter the runner beans and girolles on warm plates. Place the crispy lambs' tongues on top, and drizzle over the warm dressing from the pan.

SWEETCORN SUPPER CLUB

Sweetcorn is American through and through, and one of the New World's great vegetable gifts to the rest of us. Sweet, nutty, juicy – who doesn't love a freshly buttered cob on the side of their BBQ plate? It's a mainstay in Chinese soups. In Succotash, it's a key part of a Thanksgiving celebration in several US states. Golden corn just screams late summer and lazy days. And, of course, no trip to the cinema would be complete without popcorn.

Try to find one of the many growers who offer pick-your-own days and just taste the difference when you eat your corn that evening. As with all vegetables, the less time between picking and cooking, the better.

WHAT TO LOOK FOR:
- silky green husks that are not too dry.
- plump, moist-looking kernels.

SWEETCORN SOUP

Serves 4

Sweetcorn lives up to its billing: it's sweet. You need to balance it out with other flavours. That's where the spicy, lime-spiked crab comes in to give this silky soup a real punch.

for the crab garnish:
100g white crabmeat
1 tablespoon pine nuts,
　toasted
1 fresh red chilli,
　deseeded and chopped
squeeze of lime juice

for the soup:
4 corn on the cob,
　husks removed
1 litre water
150g butter
1 onion, finely chopped
1 garlic clove, crushed
salt and freshly ground
　black pepper

Put all the ingredients for the crab garnish into a small bowl and mix gently. Set aside.

Stand the corn cobs upright on a chopping board, and cut down as close as possible to the core to remove the sweetcorn kernels, then set them aside. Cut the cores of the sweetcorn in half and put them in a medium saucepan. Cover them with the water and bring to the boil. Simmer for 20 minutes, then strain into a jug and set aside. This gives you a nice, simple sweetcorn stock.

Melt the butter in another saucepan over a medium heat and cook the onion and garlic until soft. Add the sweetcorn kernels and season with salt and pepper. Cook for 2–3 minutes. Then cover with the sweetcorn stock. Bring it up to the boil and simmer for 8–10 minutes or until the sweetcorn is soft. Remove from the heat and blend with an immersion blender or in a food-processor until it's nice and smooth. If you're using a food-processor, let the soup cool a little before you whizz it.

Pass the soup through a fine sieve into serving bowls, and serve garnished with the crab.

SWEETCORN, CAPER & PINE NUT DRESSING WITH SEA BREAM

Serves 4

Pan-fried sea bream with a nutty, sweet-sour dressing enriched with some brown butter. A sophisticated *salade tiède*.

---

for the dressing:
30g sultanas
200g unsalted butter
30g pine nuts
juice of ½ lemon
100g cooked
　sweetcorn kernels
2–3 tablespoons capers
1 teaspoon thyme leaves

for the sea bream:
1 tablespoon
　vegetable oil
4 sea bream fillets,
　skin on
salt and freshly ground
　black pepper

Soak the sultanas in hot water for 2 hours, and then strain and set aside.

Put the butter into a large saucepan over a medium heat and bring to the boil – here, we want it to colour ever so slightly so that it has a nutty flavour. Add the pine nuts and cook until they're golden, then remove the pan from the heat. Add the lemon juice, followed by the sweetcorn, soaked sultanas, capers and thyme. Set aside and keep warm.

Heat the oil in a heavy-based frying pan over a medium heat. Season the sea bream with salt and pepper, then place in the pan, skin-side down. Cook for 5–6 minutes, then turn and cook on the other side for a further minute.

To serve, divide the sweetcorn dressing between 4 warm plates and arrange the sea bream fillets on top.

BRAISED SWEETCORN & WOOD PIGEON

Serves 4

This is one of the ultimate seasonal dishes, one that seems just as Nature intended. The pigeons eat sweetcorn, and then the sweetcorn is served with the bird. It's a classic combination of gamey flesh, salty bacon and sweet vegetables.

4 crown of wood pigeon
2 tablespoons
  vegetable oil
20 baby onions, peeled
1 carrot, peeled and
  cut into strips
2 rashers of smoked
  streaky bacon, diced
500ml good chicken stock
100g cooked sweetcorn
  kernels
50g butter
salt and freshly ground
  black pepper

Preheat the oven to 160°C/gas mark 3.

Season the pigeons well with salt and pepper. Heat a large, heavy-based, ovenproof frying pan over a medium heat. When it's hot, add 1 tablespoon of the vegetable oil. Put the pigeons into the pan and evenly brown them all over. Don't be tempted to rush this – you'll get more flavour and colour if you take your time. Transfer the pan to the oven for 10–12 minutes. Remove from the oven, take the pigeon out of the frying pan and set aside, covered, to rest for 10–15 minutes.

Blanch the baby onions and the carrot strips separately in boiling salted water, then plunge into ice-cold water to stop the cooking process. When they're cold, drain and set aside on kitchen paper to dry.

Heat another frying pan over a medium heat, add the rest of the vegetable oil and cook the bacon until crisp and golden. Add the onions and cook for a further 2 minutes. Cover the bacon and onion with the stock and bring to the boil. Add the sweetcorn and carrots, and simmer for 5 minutes. Then add the butter, stir through and season with salt and pepper to taste. Remove from the heat immediately.

To serve, remove the pigeon meat from the bone if you wish. Pour the sweetcorn and bacon mixture into a large bowl or individual servings, and arrange the pigeon on top.

POPCORN PANNACOTTA

Serves 4

Everybody loves popcorn. When we were playing around with the idea for this dessert there was an element of trial and error. We tried it first with a sweetcorn purée, but it turned out with a texture like a heavy blancmange. But then we came up with the blitzed 'popcorn powder' and we hit the jackpot. It's like space rocks for grown-ups.

---

for the popcorn:
120ml olive oil
60g icing sugar
50g popping corn

for the pannacotta:
3 gelatine leaves
550ml double cream
100ml milk
100g caster sugar

3 pinches of sea salt

Preheat the oven to 110°C/gas mark ¼.

Heat a heavy-based saucepan over a medium heat. Add the olive oil and the icing sugar and cook to a very light golden caramel. Watch it carefully! Add the popcorn and mix it well into the caramel.

When the corn starts to pop, put the lid on the pan and leave for 3–5 minutes or until the corn has all popped. When it's ready, tip the popcorn onto a baking tray, sprinkle with the sea salt, then transfer to the oven for about 5 minutes to dry out. Once it's dry, keep back a small handful to decorate and use a blender or food-processor to reduce the rest to a powder. Set aside.

Soak the gelatine in cold water and set aside until soft. Put the cream, milk and sugar in a large saucepan and bring to the boil. Remove from the heat and add the popcorn powder. Leave in a warm place for 40 minutes to infuse and extract as much of the popcorn flavour as possible.

Return the saucepan to the heat and bring the mixture back to the boil. Add the softened, squeezed-out gelatine and stir until dissolved. Pass the mixture through a fine sieve into a clean saucepan. Pour into 4 glasses and allow to cool, then transfer to the fridge to set for 1–2 hours.

To serve, turn the pannacottas out onto individual plates and decorate with the reserved popcorn.

POTATO SUPPER CLUB

Aside from fruit, nowhere are different varieties more apparent than with potatoes. There's the red-skinned and hardy Desirée, smooth and creamy-tasting; fluffy, floury King Edward and Maris Piper, both of which are terrific for roasting; waxy Charlotte, just made for salads; sweet and longingly awaited new season's Jersey Royal; long and knobbly but oh-so-flavourful Ratte… there are so many to choose from, and each one of them has their own unique flavour, texture and skill set.

For a chef with a restaurant, it's a question of consistency, so we ensure all our potatoes come from the same valued supplier. Potatoes have to be stored at a cool temperature, otherwise their starch will leach out of them before we get to cook them. They should also be kept in the dark. So we consider them the way we consider lamb or fish, we store them very carefully and treat them with the respect they deserve.

Most of the following recipes require a different type of spud – it's very important to pick the right potato for the job you want it to perform. But if you're looking for a good all-rounder, I tend to plump for Desirée. She just never lets me down.

WHAT TO LOOK FOR:
- firm potatoes with few or no blemishes; definitely no signs of sprouting.
- good colour and definitely no patches of green.

POTATO SALAD &
HORSERADISH MAYONNAISE

Serves 4

When I was developing this potato salad, I knew I wanted something a bit different – to be able to taste the potatoes and appreciate their different flavours, colours and textures without drowning them in mayonnaise. So here we go – it's a modernist structure of a dish, if I say so myself.

6 Charlotte potatoes
50ml olive oil
6 Pink Fir potatoes
200g Mayonnaise
  (see the Herb
  Mayonnaise on page
  77 and leave out
  the herbs)
50g creamed horseradish
100g mixed leaves
salt and freshly ground
  black pepper

Put the Charlotte potatoes into a pan of cold salted water. Bring to the boil and simmer for 15–20 minutes. Drain off the water, peel the Charlottes and cut into quarters. Season with salt and pepper, then drizzle with half the olive oil and set aside to keep warm.

Cut the Pink Fir potatoes into slices 1cm thick. Drop into a pan of boiling salted water and cook for about 5 minutes or until ready. Drain off the water, season with salt and pepper, drizzle with the remaining olive oil and set aside to keep warm.

Mix the mayonnaise with the horseradish in a bowl until well combined.

To serve, smear a heaped tablespoon of the horseradish mayonnaise onto a plate. Place the potatoes on top and scatter over the mixed leaves.

Bryn's Tip: To ring the changes, try an Odette's riff on a fish 'n' chips, salt 'n' vinegar flavour by deep-frying a handful of capers and scattering them over the potato salad: heat some vegetable oil in a deep-fat fryer to 180°C. Drain and thoroughly dry some capers (pat them on kitchen paper). Deep-fry them in the hot oil – stand well back as they will spit like crazy – until they're golden and have opened up like little flowers. It will take only about 30 seconds. Remove from the oil and drain the capers on kitchen paper. (If you're worried about the spitting, you can leave these out but they are delicious, and add a lovely salty crunch to the dish.)

HASH BROWN, POACHED EGG & HOLLANDAISE SAUCE

Serves 4

This Sunday brunch dish is one of the most popular with vegetarian and non-vegetarian customers alike at Odette's. The humble diner favourite is given a slick of sophistication with a homemade hollandaise and a poached egg. In fact, it's perfect for breakfast, brunch, or for supper in front of the telly.

for the hash browns:
2 shallots, peeled and finely chopped
1 tablespoon thyme leaves
approx. 150ml olive oil
2 large Desirée potatoes, washed but not peeled
100g melted butter
1–2 handfuls of rock salt, for lining a roasting tin
salt and freshly ground black pepper

1 portion of Hollandaise Sauce (see page 63), leaving out the wild garlic

for the poached eggs:
4 free range eggs
1 tablespoon vinegar
1 teaspoon salt

Preheat the oven to 180°C/gas mark 4.

Place the shallots and the thyme leaves in a saucepan, and then pour over enough olive oil so that they are just covered. Put the pan over a low heat and simmer the shallots for 20 minutes or until cooked (do not allow the oil to boil at any time). In essence, here you are using a confit method; you want the shallots to keep their integrity and structure, but to gain a sweetness. When they are ready, remove the pan from the heat and set aside.

Line a roasting tin with a layer of rock salt, no more than 2cm thick. Place the potatoes on the bed of salt (this helps to draw out their moisture) and bake in the oven for 30 minutes. When the time is up, remove the potatoes from the oven and set aside to cool sufficiently for you to handle them. Peel the potatoes then coarsely grate them into a bowl. Using a slotted spoon, add the shallot mixture to the potato, discarding the oil, and season with salt and pepper. Add the melted butter and mix together well. Set aside.

Make the hollandaise on page 63, leaving out the wild garlic, and set aside while you poach the eggs.

Poach the eggs according to the instructions on page 85.

Finally, cook the hash browns. Heat 1–2 tablespoons olive oil in a frying pan over a medium heat. When it's hot, add the potato mixture and pack it down with a spatula to about 2cm thick. Reduce the heat and cook for 4–5 minutes until golden brown. Turn over and cook for a further 4–5 minutes. When ready, remove from the frying pan and set aside on kitchen paper to drain.

To serve, quarter the hash brown and transfer to individual plates. Place the egg on top of the hash brown then cover the egg with the sauce.

CRUSHED NEW POTATOES WITH SEA TROUT, TOMATO & OLIVES

Serves 4

This dish is a herald of summer to me. The leaves of new potatoes have reared their heads above the dusty soil, tomatoes are ripening ruby red, and the sea trout are running. So we just combine what the season has given us and *voilà* – a beautiful, light lunch or dinner.

4 plum tomatoes
50ml olive oil, plus extra
    for drizzling
½ garlic clove,
    finely chopped
1 tablespoon
    chopped shallot
1 tablespoon Spiced
    Tomato Chutney
    (see page 217)
4 green olives, pitted
    and halved
4 basil leaves
400g Jersey Royal
    or Charlotte potatoes,
    washed
4 x 150g sea trout fillets,
    pin boned, skin on
salt and freshly ground
    black pepper

Blanch the tomatoes in boiling salted water for 10 seconds, then place in ice-cold water. Once cold, peel them, cut them in half and scoop out and discard the seeds. Then cut the flesh into 5mm dice.

Place the olive oil, garlic, shallot and tomato chutney in a saucepan and heat gently – do not allow it to boil. Add the olives, diced tomato and basil, and season with salt and pepper. Set aside to keep warm.

Put the potatoes into a pan of cold salted water, bring to the boil, and simmer for 15–20 minutes or until just tender. Remove from the heat and drain them through a colander. Return them to the dry pan over a low heat and remove any excess water. When dry, crush the potatoes roughly using the back of a fork. Season with salt and pepper and drizzle with olive oil to bind. Set aside to keep warm.

Score the skin of the sea trout with a sharp knife. Season the flesh of the fillets with salt and pepper. Place them, skin-side down, in a frying pan over a medium heat, add a drizzle of olive oil, and cook for 4–5 minutes. When the skin is crispy, turn off the heat, then turn over the fish to gently warm the underside in the heat of the pan.

To serve, pile the crushed potatoes in the centre of a serving plate. Put the sea trout on top of the potatoes and drizzle with the tomato and olive dressing.

WARM POTATO SALAD WITH TRUFFLES & PERL WEN

Serves 4–6

Perl Wen is a faintly lemony, creamy, rinded cheese from Wales – the perfect partner for musky truffles and warm, waxy Charlotte potatoes. You will need to start preparing this dish 2–3 days before you want to serve it.

1 small Perl Wen cheese
3 black truffles
12 Charlotte potatoes
100ml Red Wine Dressing
   (see page 216)
50g mixed leaf salad
bunch of chives, chopped
salt and freshly ground
   black pepper

Cut the cheese in half horizontally using a long thin knife. Slice the truffles as thinly as possible, and season them with salt and pepper. Spread the truffles evenly over the bottom half of the cheese and replace the top half to cover the truffles. Then wrap the cheese back in its original paper and put it in the fridge for 2–3 days to mature.

Remember to remove the cheese from the fridge at least an hour before serving.

Put the Charlotte potatoes into a pan of cold salted water, bring to the boil, and simmer for 15–20 minutes or until just tender. Drain off the water and peel the potatoes. Cut them into rounds, and season with salt and pepper. Drizzle them with 50ml of the dressing while they're still warm and set aside.

To serve, put the mixed leaves into a bowl and season with the remaining dressing. Add the chopped chives to the warm potatoes. Cut the cheese into slices and arrange on plates. Place the warm potato and dressed salad to the side.

TOMATO SUPPER CLUB

I've written a bit about varieties of vegetables in this book, but tomatoes take this to another level. There's something like 7,500 different kinds. And it doesn't stop there. I'm a big fan of heritage or heirloom tomatoes, which are often sweeter than many of the commercial hybrid varieties. Sometimes it's a bit daunting to have so much choice but, once again, the different types lend themselves to different uses in the kitchen: beefsteak and the smaller, heart-shaped ox-heart tomatoes are brilliant for slicing; plum tomatoes famously make the best Italian purées and passatas. Sweet little yellow and red cherry tomatoes are wonderful as an appetiser, simply dipped into some sea salt. And they're a great friend to the gardener too – tomatoes lend themselves to companion planting. Try planting them alongside your carrots. They really help each other out.

Tomatoes are one of the few vegetables that take well to canning, and it's always useful to have a stock of perfectly ripe cooked tinned tomatoes in your kitchen cupboards.

The one thing tomatoes require, both as a growing plant and as an ingredient, is warmth. There's nothing worse than the horrible mealiness of a tomato taken straight from the fridge – so do try to avoid that if you can! But nothing beats biting into a sun-warmed tomato straight off the vine. It's one of life's great pleasures.

WHAT TO LOOK FOR:
- heaviness for size.
- that lovely, unmistakable tomato scent when the green stalk is sniffed.
- a bright, deep colour and plumpness.

TOMATO GAZPACHO

Serves 4

I first had this soup when I was about 17 or 18, on holiday in Ibiza with my mates. It blew me away. They, on the other hand, couldn't stop laughing at me, the creative chef-to-be, for ordering cold tomato soup! I didn't care – this is GREAT tomato soup. This needs to be made the day before you want to serve it.

3 red peppers, peeled,
   deseeded and
   cut into a small dice
3 cucumbers, peeled,
   deseeded and cut
   into small dice
16 ripe tomatoes,
   halved and deseeded
1 litre passata
4 garlic cloves, peeled
3 banana shallots,
   peeled and sliced
pinch of celery salt
150ml olive oil
100ml white wine vinegar
1 teaspoon coriander
   seeds, toasted

to garnish:
1 tablespoon stoned
   black olives
1 tablespoon fresh
   basil, torn

Place all the ingredients except the olives and basil in a large bowl. Mix thoroughly, cover the bowl and place in the fridge for 24 hours.

When you're ready, blitz in a food processor or blender and then pass through a fine sieve. This is best served VERY cold, garnished with the olives and basil.

TOMATO TART & SARDINES

Serves 4

Remember picnics as a kid? We'd have sardine sandwiches and plates of tomatoes to dip into salt and munch. Well, this is just a cheffy version of that, with an added jolt of sweet shallots, thyme and crisp puff pastry.

200g puff pastry
    (shop-bought is fine)
flour, for dusting
100ml olive oil,
    plus extra for brushing
3 banana shallots,
    peeled and sliced
2 sprigs of thyme,
    leaves only
30–40 ripe cherry
    tomatoes, halved
12 black olives,
    stoned and quartered
4 butterflied fresh sardines
    or 8 fresh fillets
juice of ½ lemon
handful of basil leaves
salt and freshly ground
    black pepper

Roll out the puff pastry on a lightly floured surface to a 3mm thickness. Cut out 4 circles, about 15cm in diameter. Run the tip of your knife 1cm in from the edge of the circle, but not all the way through the pastry – this will create a little lip when the pastry rises. Then prick the inner pastry circle with a fork. Transfer the pastry to a baking sheet lined with greaseproof paper and put in the fridge to cool for at least 2 hours.

Heat the olive oil in a frying pan over a medium heat and add the shallots and thyme. Cook for about 8 minutes until the shallots are soft, without letting them colour. Season with salt and pepper. Remove from the heat and set aside to cool.

Preheat the oven to 190°C/gas mark 5. Place a baking tray in the oven to heat up.

Remove the pastry rounds from the fridge. Spread the shallot mixture over the inner circle of the rounds, and then place the tomato halves on top, packing them tightly together. Ensure that the tomatoes and the shallot mixture are arranged within the border of the puff pastry, otherwise the sides will not rise up to encase the tomatoes and their juices.

Brush the tomatoes and the edges of the puff pastry with a little olive oil and season with salt and pepper. Carefully slide the pastry circles on their greaseproof paper onto the preheated baking tray and cook for 12 minutes.

Once cooked, remove the tarts from the oven and scatter the olives over the top. Set aside to keep warm.

Preheat the grill until hot. Oil a baking tray and season it generously with salt and pepper. Place the sardines on it, flesh-side down, and pop under the grill for 2–3 minutes until the fish is cooked. Remove from the heat and squeeze over the lemon juice. To serve, place 1 sardine or 2 fillets on top of each tart, and scatter with the basil leaves.

TOMATO CONSOMMÉ &
POACHED SALMON

Serves 4

This is a little complex and it takes time to get it right – you really do want a clear, pure consommé of tomato – but it is so worth it. Light, delicious and looks beautiful on the plate.

This needs to be prepared the day before.

for the consommé:
20 ripe tomatoes, deseeded and roughly chopped
2 garlic cloves, peeled
2 sticks of celery
celery salt, to taste
white pepper, to taste
small bunch of chervil, reserving some to garnish
small bunch of basil, reserving some to garnish

for the salmon:
4 x 100g salmon supremes
6 black olives, pitted and halved
50g cooked peas
1 tomato, peeled (see page 144), deseeded and diced
drizzle of olive oil
salt and freshly ground black pepper

First make the consommé. Place all the ingredients into a large bowl and season with the celery salt and white pepper to taste. Then transfer the lot to a blender or food-processor and pulp the mixture – do not reduce it to a purée. Pour the mixture back into the bowl and leave to stand in the fridge for 3–4 hours. Pour the chilled tomato mixture into a colander lined with a muslin cloth and set over a bowl. Fold the muslin cloth over the mix and place a light weight on top to help extract the liquid. Leave in the fridge overnight.

Remove the weight, muslin and colander, discard the pulp and pour all of the liquid into a saucepan.

Season the salmon with salt and pepper and place in a steamer. Steam for 5–6 minutes or until just tender and cooked through, then transfer to a serving bowl.

Bring the tomato consommé very slowly to a simmer – do not allow it to boil. When it's warm, pour over the salmon. Add the olives, peas and tomato around the salmon, then scatter with the reserved basil and chervil, and finish with a few drops of olive oil.

GREEN TOMATO CHUTNEY & CHEESE

Makes about 1 litre

Tomatoes are a bit tricky to get a dessert, so we came up with a cheese course instead, serving it with crumbly Welsh Caerphilly. The green tomatoes in the chutney are actually a tomato variety (although I have also made this using underripe tomatoes in the past and it has worked). I love the smell of green tomatoes – it's the scent of summer.

Feel free to serve up this chutney with cold meats and salad for a light lunch or supper too.

2 onions, finely chopped
6 large green courgettes, trimmed and grated
50g fresh ginger root, grated
600g caster sugar
1 tablespoon ground allspice
1 litre cider vinegar
2kg green tomatoes, deseeded and chopped

Caerphilly, to serve

Put all the ingredients, except the tomatoes, in a large heavy-based saucepan and bring to the boil over a medium heat. Reduce the heat and simmer, stirring occasionally to prevent sticking, until the mixture has a nice jammy consistency.

Add the tomatoes and cook for 20 minutes. Remove from the heat and ladle into clean jars, sterilised by following the method on page 220. Label the jars with the date you made it. The chutney will keep for up to 6 months in the fridge.

FRUIT

FRUIT

Yes, I know – this is a vegetable book, but I felt really strongly that we had to have a chapter on fruit (and, technically speaking, rhubarb is a vegetable and the tomato is a fruit). Orchards and their produce play a huge part in our landscape, our heritage as well as our food. Wherever you are reading this: please, try to buy locally grown varieties whenever you can. Our orchards are disappearing.

Fruit played a huge part in my life as a boy growing up in Denbigh: there was a gnarled apple tree from which we used to scrump the fruit for our apple fights; there were local plums baked into warming crumbles and pies by my Nan; there were pears, sliced and eaten raw with a beautiful piece of Caerphilly cheese whilst shooting with Dad and my uncle. Anyone growing up on or near a farm will know what I mean when I say that, before we knew about our 'five-a-day', we were eating at least that amount in seasonal fruits alone.

Alongside the fruit I grew up with, my two other absolute favourites – ones that always, always grace my kitchens, both professional and at home – have got to be the glorious, juicy and ever so saucy cherry, and, although not from British shores, the mighty lemon. I can't imagine a kitchen without lemons, many a dish would be lacklustre without it. The sour fruit with slightly bitter skin from distant parts of the world has entered the mainstream of British cooking and become a staple. Bloody marvellous!

As with vegetables, treat your fruit with respect. A heck of a lot has gone into growing that apple, pear or cherry. From planting the seedlings to building the orchard, fruit can take 3–10 years to develop. Think about that the next time you bite into a beautiful fresh apple, or stew some damsons.

Take your time. Choose your produce with care. And enjoy the bounty.

RHUBARB SUPPER CLUB

The thing with rhubarb is that you need quite a lot of sugar to make it sweet. Once its tartness is suitably tamed, as in crumbles and fools, it is something of a British dessert classic. So when we used it for our second Supper Club, it was the first three courses that took up most of my attention. That inherent sharpness means rhubarb becomes a foil to oily ingredients, like the mackerel and duck we're using in this selection. And it adds a shock of vibrant colour to the plate.

I prefer to use forced rhubarb wherever possible. Forcing rhubarb gives it a much better flavour. It is less astringent, and the tender, bright pink stems are more consistent in quality. Farmers grow the rootstock outside for up to three years to ensure it's strong and healthy before moving it into dark growing sheds. (Inside, you can hear the plants crack as they grow, struggling for the light.) The plants thrive in the cold – rhubarb originates from China and Siberia – which makes them ideally suited to the British climate! In the 19th century, 90 per cent of the world's forced rhubarb came from the so-called Rhubarb Triangle in West Yorkshire. Small wonder, then, that rhubarb is one of our favourite ingredients.

WHAT TO LOOK FOR:
- firm, thick stems and good vibrant colour.
- you want crisp stems that release sap when snapped – avoid any limp or slimy ones.

RHUBARB, BEETROOT & WHIPPED GOAT'S CHEESE SALAD

Serves 4

Here, I'm using bright pink rhubarb with its slightly sweetened sourness to cut through the rich, creamy cheese in a simple yet delicious starter.

2 golden beetroots, trimmed

200g trimmed rhubarb, forced if available, cut into 2cm pieces

juice of 1 orange

4 black peppercorns

1 sprig of thyme

100g sugar

250ml olive oil

200g soft goat's cheese

100ml double cream

50g crème fraîche

large handful of rocket

salt and freshly ground black pepper

Preheat the oven to 160°C/gas mark 3. Wrap the beetroots individually in foil and put into a roasting tin. Bake in the oven for 2 hours.

20 minutes before the end of this time, put the rhubarb, orange juice, peppercorns, thyme and sugar into a second roasting tin and put in the oven for 10–15 minutes, or until the rhubarb is soft. Drain off the liquid into a bowl and then whisk in the olive oil to make a dressing.

When the beetroots are cooked, remove them from the oven and set aside to cool, still wrapped – they will steam a little in the foil, and this helps you to peel them easily. Once cool, peel the beetroot, and cut into 8. Season the pieces with salt.

Put the goat's cheese into a food-processor fitted with a paddle (or a large mixing bowl if you have a hand-held beater) and beat for 2 minutes. Pour in the double cream and crème fraîche, and beat again until thick and smooth.

To serve, arrange the rhubarb and the beetroot on a large plate. Spoon on the goat's cheese, scatter the rocket leaves on top, then pour over the dressing.

SPICED RHUBARB & MACKEREL

Serves 4

Both mackerel and rhubarb take well to spices. Indeed, they take well to each other, too – the sharpness and acidity of the rhubarb cutting through the richness of the fish. This is a really healthy dish, full of Omega 3 fatty acids and vitamin C.

---

2 tablespoons
  vegetable oil
4 mackerel fillets,
4 rhubarb stems,
  cut into 2cm pieces
pinch of ground allspice
splash of sherry vinegar
75g sugar
salt and freshly ground
  black pepper

Heat a large frying pan over a medium heat and add the oil. When it's hot, add the mackerel fillets, skin-side down, and season the flesh with salt and pepper. Cook for 3–4 minutes, and then turn over for a further minute to finish. Remove the fish from the pan and set aside to keep warm.

Add the rhubarb, allspice and vinegar to the same pan. Reduce the heat and cook gently for about 1 minute. Add the sugar and cook until the rhubarb is soft, about 3–4 minutes.

To serve, divide the rhubarb between 4 plates and top with the mackerel fillets, flesh-side down. Season with salt to taste.

RHUBARB TART & CONFIT DUCK LEG

Serves 4

Rich duck is complemented by tart rhubarb. This pairing is fairly traditional in Europe. I have simply taken what would normally be served as a sweet-sour, pink sauce and wrapped it in a flaky parcel to sit alongside the duck.

The duck legs are best started the day before you want to serve the dish.

---

6 rhubarb stems,
   about 24cm long
100g puff pastry
   (shop-bought is fine)
1 tablespoon honey
handful of chopped
   pistachio nuts
good pinch of salt
4 Confit Duck legs
   (see page 70)

Cut the rhubarb stems in half. Roll out the pastry into a rectangle that is 2cm wider and longer than your sticks of rhubarb when they are lined up in a row (see picture). Prick the pastry all over with a fork – this will help prevent it from bubbling up as it cooks. Place on a baking tray and pop in the fridge to rest for 1 hour.

Preheat the oven to 180°C/gas mark 4.

Place the rhubarb on the pastry, then fold in the edges around the rhubarb to keep it compactly in place. Put the tart in the oven for 15 minutes until the pastry has cooked. Remove from the oven and brush the rhubarb all over with some of the honey. Return to the oven for 4–5 minutes, until the pastry is golden and the rhubarb is cooked. Then remove from the oven, and brush with the remaining honey. Sprinkle with the chopped pistachio nuts and the sea salt and set aside.

To serve, remove the duck legs from the fat and place them under a hot grill to crisp up the fat. Cut the rhubarb tart into 4, place on plates and serve a duck leg on each slice.

RHUBARB FOOL

Serves 4

Who doesn't love a fool? A classic British dessert, my version is flavoured with stem ginger, cardamom and star anise to spice it up.

500g trimmed
  rhubarb, chopped
120g sugar
1 cardamom pod
1 star anise
1 teaspoon stem ginger,
  finely chopped
300ml double cream
100ml natural yogurt

Put the rhubarb in a large saucepan with 100g of the sugar. Add the cardamom pod and star anise. Bring to a simmer, then place a lid on the pan for 2–3 minutes, just to release the water from the rhubarb. Remove the lid, add the stem ginger, and simmer until the rhubarb is soft. Remove from the heat and set aside to cool.

Whip the cream in a large bowl with the remaining sugar until it forms soft peaks. Fold in the yogurt. Set aside until the rhubarb has cooled.

Remove the star anise and the cardamom pod from the cooled rhubarb.

To serve, divide the rhubarb mixture between 4 serving glasses, spoon on some of the whipped cream, and drizzle over any remaining pink cooking juices.

APPLES

Britain is famous for its apples – we have more than twelve hundred varieties. They are, I maintain, my favourite of all the autumn fruits. And yet, as a British chef, I feel we still don't make enough of them. Nothing beats biting into a fresh and perfect apple, straight from the tree. At Odette's, we have apples on the menu in one form or another throughout the year.

Originally, apples came from Kazakhstan in Central Asia, where they still grow wild today. Their apples span the entire flavour spectrum we know in the West. So I suppose you could, if you wanted, go back to the source to create your own brand new apple variety from scratch. Maybe I should!

There are different types of apple for every job. You would never eat a cider apple, for example, nor press a Bramley cooking apple to make cider. Apart from considerations of flavour, some varieties are crisp and firm textured, lending themselves to use in open, French-style tarts, whereas others are soft, more easily broken down on cooking, and so perfect for sauce. So, once again, in these apple recipes I have specified which I think are best suited to their given role.

WHAT TO LOOK FOR:
* firm apples, with no bruises, soggy patches, or split or insect-damaged skins.

APPLE SAUCE

Serves 6–8

Sweet and tart apple sauce is one of my favourite things and it's so simple to make – you will never buy it in a jar again.

4 Bramley apples,
   peeled, quartered
   and cored
1 tablespoon caster sugar

Roughly chop three of the apples into a large saucepan. Grate the remaining apple and add that to the pan. Add the sugar, and cook over a medium heat for about 10 minutes, stirring occasionally until the apples are cooked through and have broken up nicely. Remove from the heat and set aside until you want to serve.

Bryn's tip: If you like your apple sauce smooth, once cooked, you can blitz it in a food-processor or blender.

APPLE & BLACKBERRY CRUMBLE

Serves 4–6

Homely, comforting and tasty: you cannot beat a delicious autumnal crumble. This one's a British classic. By keeping the berries whole, you give the filling wonderful bursts of flavour in the cooked dish.

for the filling:
12 Cox's or Bramley apples,
   peeled and cored
125g caster sugar
250g blackberries,
   kept whole

for the crumble:
250g plain flour
200g caster sugar
200g butter,
   straight from the fridge
150g flaked almonds

Preheat the oven to 160°C/gas mark 3.

Cut 3 of the apples into small dice, and put in a heavy-based saucepan with the sugar. Add enough water to just cover the apples and cook over a low heat, stirring occasionally, until soft. Depending on your apples, this should take 5 minutes or so – keep checking. Remove from the heat and, using the back of a fork, break down the cubes into a rough mash, and set aside.

Cut the remaining apples into bite-sized pieces, making them as uniform as possible. Add these apples to the cooked apple and mix them well. Then add the blackberries to the apple mix and set aside.

To make the crumble, mix the flour and sugar together in a large bowl. Then add the butter in small pieces, rubbing it into the flour and sugar using the tips of your fingers until it forms a crumbly mixture, a bit like rough breadcrumbs. Add the flaked almonds and mix them through. Tip the crumble mix onto a baking tray, spread out evenly, and cook in the oven until the mixture is golden brown, about 10 minutes. This will ensure a good crispy crumble topping.

Pour the apple and blackberry mix into a large pie dish and cover with the cripsy crumble mix. Cook in the oven for a further 10 minutes.

Bryn's Tip: I've suggested Cox's or Bramley apples here but try seeking out one of our old, rare varieties, the Norfolk Biffin. It was prized as a cooking apple in Victorian times, and was a real favourite of the great cookery writer Eliza Acton.

THIN APPLE TART

Serves 4

Thin slices of crisp tart apple set against a background of soft frangipane, fragrant with almonds. Serve as dessert, with morning coffee or afternoon tea: you choose.

200g puff pastry
(shop-bought is fine)
flour, for dusting
8 Braeburn apples, cored,
peeled and finely sliced
50g Frangipane
(about a quarter of the
recipe on page 182)
50g butter, melted, plus
extra for greasing
50g caster sugar

Roll out the puff pastry on a lightly floured surface to a 3mm thickness. Cut out 4 circles, about 15cm in diameter. Run the tip of your knife 1cm in from the edge of each circle, but not all the way through the pastry – this will create a little lip when the pastry rises. Then prick the pastry of the inner circle with a fork. Transfer them to a lightly greased baking sheet and put in the fridge to cool for at least 2 hours.

Preheat the oven to 180°C/gas mark 4.

Remove the pastry from the fridge. Spread the frangipane over the inner circles, then arrange the apple slices on top, overlapping the slices clockwise until you can tuck the final apple slice under the first one. Brush with the melted butter then sprinkle with the sugar.

Bake in the oven for 20 minutes, or until the pastry is cooked and golden.

Serve with ice cream or cream.

CHERRIES

I love cherries. There's something special about them. And how utterly romantic is the sight of cherry trees in blossom in spring. Whenever I see them, they fill me with optimism for the coming fruit. And, once the pruning's done in the autumn, all those cherry wood trimmings are brilliant for smoking meat and fish, or for building a cooking fire in its own right.

I remember when I started cheffing in Provence I was given the job of stoning all the cherries for that evening's clafoutis: well, by the end of the day I was so spattered with blood-red juices that I looked like an extra from a horror movie! You can always tell which poor commis was given that task…

Cherries are at their best in high summer. That's when their flavour is at its most intense, and their colours range from a yellowy pink to a deep garnet, and almost to black. At Le Gavroche, to take advantage of this incredible ruby bounty, we would serve large bowls of cherries, stem on, in chilled bowls. Just pure, simple stone-fruit heaven. Try to eat local cherries. Please! We are losing some of our indigenous varieties, and our cherry farmers need your support.

WHAT TO LOOK FOR:
- cherries sold on their stems – they should be plump, glossy and full of juice.
- avoid any bruised or flaccid fruit.

CHERRY CLAFOUTIS

Serves 4

Baked sweet custard studded with fresh, tart cherries bursting with garnet juices – this version of the traditional French dessert is an absolute stunner. It is best served with a dash of cream – too much and you will drown out those flavours.

40g butter, melted and
  cooled, plus extra
  for greasing
50g plain flour
70g caster sugar
200ml double cream
3 free range eggs
300g cherries,
  stoned and halved

Preheat the oven to 160°C/gas mark 3. Grease a 20cm cake tin or individual tart tins with butter.

Sift the flour into a large bowl. Add the sugar and mix them together. Pour in the cream, followed by the eggs, and stir well. Finish the batter by adding the melted butter and stir well until everything is combined.

Scatter the cherries evenly over the base of the cake tin or tins. Pour the batter over the fruit and bake until golden and risen – about 30 minutes for a large one, or 8–12 minutes for individual tins.

Serve warm.

POACHED CHERRIES & CHOCOLATE SORBET

Serves 4

With deep, red cherries, verging on black, coupled with wickedly dark chocolate sorbet, this sexy combination has an element of that seventies classic Black Forest Gateau. I've simply brought it up to date.

for the poached cherries:
100g butter
175g sugar
500g cherries, stoned
200ml red wine
juice and zest of
  ½ orange
½ vanilla pod
50g chopped pistachios,
  to garnish

for the chocolate sorbet:
200g dark chocolate
  (minimum 64% cocoa
  solids), broken into
  pieces
800ml water
200ml milk
80ml glucose syrup
250g caster sugar
60g cocoa powder

Put the butter and sugar in a heavy-based saucepan. Heat gently until the mixture starts to bubble, then add the cherries and stir well. Add the red wine, orange juice and zest, followed by the vanilla pod. Bring everything to a simmer, then remove from the heat and set aside to cool.

To make the chocolate sorbet, put the chocolate into a large bowl. Put the water, milk, glucose syrup, sugar and cocoa powder into a large saucepan over a medium heat and bring to the boil. Then pour it onto the chocolate and whisk or stir to melt the chocolate. Continue until the mixture is really smooth and glossy then set aside to cool.

When completely cold, pour the mixture into an ice-cream machine, and churn until ready. Then place in the freezer until needed.

Remember to transfer your ice cream from the freezer to the fridge about 20 minutes before you want to eat it.

To serve, retrieve the vanilla pod from the saucepan and spoon the cherries and their poaching juices into shallow bowls. Top each serving with a scoop of the chocolate sorbet and finish with the chopped pistachios.

PEARS

Just as a piece of meat should be properly hung, fruit must be properly ripe. And ripe pear is a delight: its scented, slightly grainy flesh, dripping with juice, is perfect with a wedge of cheese. Pear and chocolate is an acknowledged match, and the sweetness of pear is enhanced with a little warming spice. Fresh or cooked, pears are fantastic. The only requirement is that the fruit must be ripe. An unripe pear is about as pleasing to eat as a brick. Pears tend to be picked unripe to prevent insect damage. So if you're unlucky enough to have some that meet that description, put them next to your bananas and they will come to ripeness that bit quicker.

As with apples, the different varieties of pear suit different jobs in the kitchen. Of the pears we regularly use, Comice pears are often thought to be the best: sweet, scented and less grainy in texture than some varieties. They're great with cheese, or just enjoyed in their own right. The Conference is the classic British eating pear. And the Williams or Bartlett pear – famously used to make the liqueur Poire Williams – is a great all-rounder, for baking as well as eating.

WHAT TO LOOK FOR:
- avoid bruising, all signs of insect damage and wrinkling of the skins.
- look for pears that are firm.
- to check for ripeness, press the skin beside the stem, it should yield gently.

SPICED POACHED PEARS & PERL LAS CHEESE

Serves 4

Perl Las is a blue cheese from Caerphilly in Wales. Its salty, tangy flavour is a superb match for these sweet, spicy pears.

1 bottle (75cl) of red wine
125g sugar
1 star anise
1 cinnamon stick
1 clove
1 cardamom pod
4 Conference pears, peeled and cored
300g Perl Las cheese

Put the wine, sugar and all the spices into a large, heavy-based saucepan. Bring to the boil, and simmer for 5 minutes. Then remove from the heat and set aside to cool. When the wine is cold, add the pears to the saucepan. Return it to the heat, bring to a gentle simmer, and poach until tender. Remove from the heat and set aside to allow the pears to cool in the spicy liquor.

When the pears are cold, serve them alongside a good piece of the Perl Las cheese.

Bryn's Tip: If you cannot get Perl Las, use a good blue cheese such as Roquefort, Stilton or Gorgonzola instead.

BRITISH PEAR TART TATIN

Serves 4

A British take on the French classic, but this time with pears. Comice are among the sweetest and juiciest of pears and hold their shape beautifully when cooked. The star anise buried in the butter gives a subtle hint of spice.

You need to prepare the pears the day before you want to serve it.

---

4 Comice pears
70g unsalted butter
2 star anise
70g sugar
100g puff pastry
   (shop-bought is fine)
flour, for dusting

Peel, core and quarter the pears, and leave them in the fridge overnight to dry out. They will discolour slightly, but don't worry – we're going to cook them.

Preheat the oven to 160°C/gas mark 3.

Spread the butter evenly over the base of a 20cm ovenproof frying pan and press the star anise into it. Then cover evenly with the sugar, and arrange the pears on top, cut-side up.

Roll out the puff pastry on a lightly floured board to 3mm thickness, trying to keep the shape as circular as possible; it should end up larger in circumference than the pan with the pears. Lay the pastry over the pears, tucking in any excess between the pears and the pan.

Place the pan over a medium heat for 5–6 minutes to start the process of caramelising the pears, then transfer the pan to the oven for 40 minutes or until the top is golden brown and oozing stickiness. Remove from the oven and set aside for about 5 minutes to cool a little.

Put a large upturned plate over the pan and carefully invert the pan and plate together so that the tart drops down onto the plate (do this quickly, as the caramelised juices are very hot). Retrieve and discard the star anise. Serve warm with good vanilla ice cream.

PEAR & ALMOND TART

Serves 4–6

This classic French tart is often called a *Tarte Bourdaloue*. Some say it's named after the Rue Bourdaloue in Paris, where the patisserie that first created this tart was once located. Whatever the origin, it is a delicious end to a meal.

for the pears:
1 litre water
350g caster sugar
1 cinnamon stick
4 Williams pears,
    peeled and cored

for the pastry:
225g plain flour, plus
    extra for dusting
140g cold unsalted butter,
    cut into small dice, plus
    extra for greasing
pinch of salt
75g caster sugar
2 free range eggs
egg wash, to glaze

for the frangipane:
250g unsalted butter,
    at room temperature
250g caster sugar
4 free range eggs
25g ground almonds
50g plain flour

1 heaped tablespoon
    apricot jam, to glaze

First poach the pears. Put the water, sugar and cinnamon stick in a large, heavy-based saucepan over a medium heat and bring to a simmer. Add the pears and poach until tender, about 10–15 minutes. Set them aside to cool in the liquid.

Now make the pastry. Mix the flour, butter, salt and sugar together in a large bowl. Add the eggs, and bring everything together very quickly to form a dough. Remove from the bowl, wrap in clingfilm and place in the fridge for 4 hours before using.

Lightly grease a 23cm tart tin with a removable base. Roll out the dough on a lightly floured work surface to a thickness of about 5mm. Carefully line the tart tin with the pastry. Leave any excess pastry hanging over the edge of the tin – this will help the tart to keep its shape, and it can be easily trimmed off after cooking. Set the pastry case aside to rest in the fridge for 40 minutes.

Preheat the oven to 180°C/gas mark 4. Line the case with greaseproof paper and fill with baking beans. Then bake in the oven for 20 minutes. Remove from the oven, lift out the paper and baking beans, and return the tart case to the oven for a further 5–7 minutes until golden brown. Remove from the oven and brush the egg wash over the pastry while it's still hot. Lower the oven temperature to 160°C/gas mark 3.

Now make the frangipane. Cream the butter and sugar together in a large bowl until pale. Then add the eggs, one at a time, plus a little of the almonds and flour with each addition. Finally add the rest of the almonds and flour, folding it in until you have a smooth mixture. Set aside to rest.

Remove the pears from their liquid and place them on kitchen paper to dry. Then carefully halve them lengthways, and then slice them lengthways again, ensuring they keep their shape. Set aside.

Fill the pastry case with the frangipane to about three-quarters full (you may not need it all). Arrange the sliced pears, flat-side down, in the frangipane and score lightly. Transfer the tart to the oven and cook for 40 minutes, or until risen and golden. Remove from the oven and set aside to cool slightly. Trim off any excess pastry.

Gently melt the apricot jam in a small saucepan over a low heat. While the tart is still warm, brush the surface with the jam to glaze. Serve on a plate at room temperature.

PLUMS

Every Welshman and woman is proud of their roots. As a chef from Denbigh, I'd say I'm a little bit prouder than most because my home town has its own variety of plum. How many people can say that?

According to one story, this plum was introduced by the Romans. I don't know if that's true or not, but what is certain is that our Denbigh plum was first recorded as a separate variety in the late 1780s. We had a tree next to my uncle's farmhouse and I loved a crumble made with its round, deliciously sweet purple-red fruit.

The Denbigh plum's story is typical of many of the world's rarer local fruit varieties. As our shopping habits have changed, and we buy more and more produce from supermarkets, there has been less and less demand for types of fruit that they don't stock. It doesn't make sense for the supermarkets to single out something specific (as they might with the Jersey Royal potato) unless people are asking for it. So in turn the farmer is less likely to grow something for which there is no demand. The Denbigh was dying out. It has taken a concerted effort to bring it back. In 2010, the Cae Dai Trust gave land for a dedicated orchard, it was planted with stock from local fruit expert Ian Sturrock, and Denbigh now hosts an annual Denbigh Plum Festival to celebrate its unique fruit.

WHAT TO LOOK FOR:
- good, even colour; a 'hand feel' somewhere between firm and slightly giving.
- avoid any fruit that are too soft, or blemished.

GLAZED DENBIGH PLUMS, BARA BRITH & HONEYCOMB ICE CREAM

Serves 4–6

This dish is a marriage of some of my favourite and most familiar things: my Nain's Bara Brith, our local Denbigh plums and honeyed ice cream. You can make the ice cream the day before you plan to serve this if you like.

for the honeycomb:
50g honey
125g glucose syrup
60ml water
325g caster sugar
1 tablespoon bicarbonate
   of soda

for the ice cream:
4 free range egg yolks
500ml milk
350g double cream
180g honeycomb pieces
   (see above)

for the plums:
juice of 1 orange
pinch of dried
   lavender buds
1 star anise
100g honey
200ml water
10 Denbigh or Victoria
   plums, halved
   and stoned

for the topping:
50ml vegetable oil
2 slices of Bara Brith
   (see page 215), cut
   into 1cm cubes

First make the honeycomb. Put the honey, glucose, water and sugar in a heavy-based saucepan and bring to the boil until a golden caramel forms. Remove from the heat and whisk in the bicarbonate of soda. Pour out onto a baking tray lined with parchment paper and set aside to cool and set. When cold, break the honeycomb into pieces.

To make the ice cream, whisk the egg yolks in a large bowl until thick and creamy. Put the milk, cream and 180g honeycomb into a heavy-based saucepan and bring to the boil over a low heat, stirring to ensure that the honeycomb melts. Pour the hot milk mixture onto the egg yolk mixture, stirring continuously to combine. Return the mixture to the cleaned saucepan over a low heat and stir until the mixture thickens sufficiently to coat the back of a spoon. Strain the mixture through a fine sieve into a bowl and mix thoroughly. Leave it to cool and then chill in the fridge.

Once cold, pour the chilled mixture into your ice-cream machine and churn until frozen, but not too stiff. Put into a suitable container and freeze until you are ready to use. Remember to transfer your ice cream from the freezer to the fridge about 20 minutes before you want to eat it.

Preheat the oven to 180°C/gas mark 4. Put the orange juice, lavender, star anise, honey and water into a small saucepan. Bring to the boil and simmer for 3–4 minutes – you don't want this taking any colour.

Place the plums cut-side up into a roasting tin, pour on the flavoured syrup and bake in the oven for 4–6 minutes or until the fruit is just soft and lightly caramelised. Remove from the oven and set aside to keep warm.

Heat the oil in a heavy-based frying pan. Add the cubes of Bara Brith and cook until golden and crispy but not dry. Remove using a slotted spoon and set aside on kitchen paper to cool.

To serve, divide the plums between bowls. Drizzle the caramel juices from the roasting tin over the fruit, and crumble over the Bara Brith. Serve with a big scoop of Honeycomb Ice Cream.

POACHED PLUMS &
YOGURT PANNACOTTA

Serves 4

Pannacotta is always a popular choice for dessert. This one has a particularly silken feel to it, and the acidity of the yogurt sits well against the sweetness of poached plums.

for the poached plums:
250ml water
100g sugar
½ cinnamon stick
½ vanilla pod
6 Victoria plums, stoned
    and cut into quarters

for the pannacotta:
3 gelatine leaves
250ml double cream
100g caster sugar
1 vanilla pod
250g natural yogurt

Start with the plums. Put the water, sugar, cinnamon stick and vanilla pod into a heavy-based saucepan. Bring to the boil and simmer for 2–3 minutes. Then add the plums and simmer until tender. Taste at this point: if the plums seem a little sour, add a bit more sugar. When they're tender, remove from the heat, and set aside to cool in the liquid.

Now for the pannacotta. Put the gelatine in a little cold water and set aside to soak until soft. Put the cream, sugar and vanilla pod in a large, heavy-based saucepan over a medium heat and bring to the boil. As soon as it's boiling, remove from the heat and take out the vanilla pod.

Squeeze the excess water from the softened gelatine and add it to the hot cream mixture. Stir well until the gelatine has fully dissolved. Put the yogurt in a separate bowl, pour in the cream mixture and whisk together until well combined. Strain the mixture through a fine sieve, and pour into 4 ramekins or glasses. Set aside to cool then transfer to the fridge to set – this should take about 2 hours.

Remove the pannacotta from the fridge and serve with the plums and a little of their poaching liquid on top.

LEMONS

I think you'll find lemons in the kitchen of every household that cooks regularly. I certainly cannot imagine mine being without them, at home or Odette's. They add freshness and brightness, and have a glorious scent.

Along with vinegars, lemons also offer you acidity, a vital component in seasoning. We tend to think of seasoning as simply being salt and pepper, but there's so much more to it than that. Seasoning is the structure on which we build flavour – and acidity, which makes you salivate and so primes the mouth, is key.

Happily, nowadays fresh lemons are available all year round. We don't have to resort to those squeezy bottles of lemon juice we used to squirt onto pancakes! I always use unwaxed lemons. The benefit of unwaxed skins is that the zest, and the oils it contains, is purer and untainted. The downside is that, without the protective wax, lemons ripen a bit faster. But that hardly matters: these beautiful fruit lend themselves so well to both savoury and sweet cooking that they're not going to hang around for long.

WHAT TO LOOK FOR:
- a lemon should feel firm and heavy for its size – a sign it's packed with juice.
- there are thin, smooth-skinned lemons and knobbly Amalfi types: make sure in both cases that the skin is unblemished and does not look tired and old.

LEMON CURD

Makes 400–600ml

juice of 4 lemons
100g unsalted butter, cut into cubes
300g sugar
4 free range eggs, beaten

Lemony, creamy and rich – this is one jar that doesn't stay full for very long in the Williams's fridge!

Put the lemon juice, butter and sugar in a heatproof bowl over a saucepan of barely simmering water, ensuring that the water does not touch the base of the bowl. Stir until the butter has melted and the sugar has dissolved. Then add the beaten eggs and cook gently, whisking occasionally, until the mixture thickens sufficiently to coat the back of a spoon. Ladle into clean jars, sterilised by following the method on page 220 while the curd is still warm. Seal, and set aside to cool completely.

Bryn's Tip: This will keep for up to 1 month in the fridge.

LEMON & POLENTA CAKE

Serves 6–8

This cake just invokes sunshine to me. Polenta is a great vehicle for lemon, soaking up all that flavour yet retaining some texture and bite.

225g softened unsalted butter, plus extra for greasing
225g caster sugar
225g ground almonds
1 vanilla pod, seeds only
3 free range eggs
juice and zest of 2 lemons
225g polenta
2 teaspoons baking powder
pinch of salt

Preheat the oven to 160°C/gas mark 3. Lightly grease a 23cm cake tin with a removable base.

Cream together the butter and sugar in a large bowl. Stir in the ground almonds and the seeds scraped from the vanilla pod. Gradually beat in the eggs, one at a time. Then add the lemon juice and zest. Fold in the polenta, together with the baking powder and salt. Pour the mixture into the cake tin and transfer to the oven for 45–55 minutes until risen and fragrant.

Remove from the oven and leave to cool in the tin for 5 minutes before turning out onto a wire rack to cool.

LEMON CURD PARFAIT & STRAWBERRIES

Serves 6

Rich, creamy, luxurious with the sharp tang of lemon curd, this one really is an exceptional end to a meal! Pâté à bombe is a French term for a light sugar syrup and egg yolk mixture used as a base for mousses and parfaits.

This needs to be made the day before you need it, and you also need a sugar thermometer for this recipe.

for the pâté à bombe:
200g caster sugar
50ml water
5 free range eggs yolks

for the lemon curd parfait:
300g Lemon Curd
  (see page 190)
juice of 1 lemon
160ml double cream,
  lightly whipped
160g pâté à bombe
  (see above)

to serve:
250g strawberries,
  hulled and halved
2 tablespoons caster sugar

First make the pâté à bombe. Put the sugar and water in a large saucepan over a medium heat to dissolve the sugar. Bring to the boil and place a sugar thermometer into the pan.

Meanwhile, put the egg yolks into the bowl of an electric mixer fitted with the whisk attachment, and beat until thick and creamy.

Keep an eye on the sugar thermometer: when it reaches 120°C, remove the pan from the heat. With the mixer still running, pour the hot syrup onto the egg yolks and continue to beat until you have a creamy, yellow cloud. This should take about 4–5 minutes. Set aside to cool, whisking every now and then until the pâté à bombe is completely cold.

Mix the lemon curd and half of the lemon juice together in a large clean bowl. Gently fold in the whipped cream. Then gently fold in the pâté à bombe, ensuring you keep the mixture nice and light. Pour into 6 ramekins and place in the freezer overnight.

Put the strawberries in a bowl, sprinkle with the sugar and squeeze over the remaining lemon juice. Set aside to steep for 1 hour.

To serve, remove the ramekins from the freezer and, using a warmed round-bladed knife, ease the parfaits out onto plates. Alternatively you can serve the parfaits in the ramekins. Decorate with the strawberries.

LEMON TART

Serves 8

Ever since my last book came out, friends and customers have been requesting other recipes to be included if I ever wrote a second book. By far the most popular request was for a lemon tart, specifically THIS lemon tart, which we serve at Odette's. It's rich, smooth, creamy and bursting with lemony flavour. A classic. This needs to be started the day before.

5 lemons
380g caster sugar
9 free range eggs
250ml double cream
unsalted butter, for
  greasing
1 quantity Sweet Pastry
  (see page 219)
flour, for dusting
egg wash, to glaze
icing sugar, to dust

Juice the lemons into a large bowl. Add the sugar and stir until dissolved.

Crack the eggs into a separate bowl and break the yolks with a large spoon. Add the double cream and mix together loosely – but don't overbeat the eggs. Pour the mixture onto the sugar and lemon juice, and mix well. Do not overmix, though: you want a cohesive yet loose mass.

Pass the mixture through a fine sieve – do not force it – and set aside to rest overnight in the fridge.

Preheat the oven to 180°C/gas mark 4 and lightly grease a 23cm tart tin.

Remove the pastry from the fridge. Roll out on a lightly floured work surface to a thickness of about 5mm, then use it to line the tart tin. Leave any excess pastry hanging over the edge of the tin – this will help it to keep its shape, and can easily be trimmed off after cooking. Leave the pastry case to rest in the fridge for 40 minutes.

Line the pastry case with greaseproof paper and fill with baking beans. Then bake in the oven for 20 minutes. Remove the tart case from the oven, lift out the paper and baking beans, and return the tart case to the oven for 5–7 minutes until the pastry is golden brown. Remove from the oven and brush beaten egg wash over the pastry while it's still hot. This will help to seal the pastry.

Reduce the oven temperature to 120°C/gas mark ½.

Set the tart case on a shelf in the oven, then pour in the lemon mixture right up to the top. Cook for 30–40 minutes, or until it just sets. The middle should wobble like a jelly. Remove from the oven and leave to cool for 3 hours at room temperature.

When cool, trim off the excess pastry and carefully remove the tart from the tin. Dust with icing sugar and caramelise lightly using a blowtorch. Cut into wedges to serve.

HERBS

HERBS

Nothing beats the scent and flavour of freshly picked herbs. One of the reasons I've always wanted to plant a herb garden at Odette's (honestly, I will get around to it) is that there aren't many things better for a chef than strolling outside to gather the herbs for a dish, straight from the plant.

Herbs form the backbone of cooking, providing depth and aroma, and giving a dish structure. I've always maintained that they're the backdrop to the main event. And I encourage you to be brave and to experiment with herbs across your cooking. Elizabeth David famously said that the use of herbs was a matter of taste and prejudice. There's no reason for not using bay leaf or basil in ice cream or lavender and rosemary with chicken. But it's only by trying things out that you'll find the combinations you prefer.

In this chapter, though, I have taken a few of them and made them the stars of their own show.

BAY LEAF ICE CREAM

Makes about 2 litres

Bay leaves have been a traditional British flavouring in sweet and savoury custards for centuries. They add a subtle scent and spice, far removed from our modern obsession with vanilla.

1.5 litres milk
450ml double cream
6 bay leaves
8 egg yolks
450g vanilla sugar

Pour the milk and double cream into a heavy-based saucepan over a low heat. Add the bay leaves and bring to the boil. Then remove the pan from the heat immediately, and set aside for 10 minutes to allow the bay leaves to infuse the liquid.

Whisk the egg yolks with the vanilla sugar in a clean bowl until thick and creamy. Set aside. When the bay has infused the cream and milk, return the saucepan to the heat and bring back to the boil. Pour the hot milk onto the egg yolk mixture, stirring continuously.

Return the mixture to the cleaned saucepan and stir, still over a low heat, until the mixture thickens sufficiently to coat the back of a spoon. Strain the mixture through a fine sieve, and stir well until thoroughly mixed. Leave it to cool and then chill in the fridge until completely cold.

Once cold, pour the chilled mixture into your ice-cream machine and churn until frozen, but not too stiff. Put into a suitable container and freeze until you are ready to use. Remember to transfer your ice cream from the freezer to the fridge about 20 minutes before you want to eat it.

LAVENDER CRÈME BRÛLÉE

Serves 6

Lavender is one of those herbs that many people think is grown only for its scent. But that wonderful aroma can play a role in cooking too, particularly in dishes from the south of France. I think it works very well in a crème brûlée. Traditionally, you would use vanilla for this. But if you use lavender instead, you create something fragrant and special.

400ml double cream
100ml milk
1 teaspoon fresh herb lavender
8 egg yolks
75g caster sugar, plus extra for sprinkling

Preheat the oven to 120°C/gas mark ½.

Pour the double cream and milk into a saucepan over a medium heat. Add the lavender and bring to the boil. Then remove the pan immediately from the heat and set aside for 10 minutes to infuse.

Meanwhile, whisk the egg yolks with the caster sugar in a large bowl until pale, thick and creamy. Pour the hot cream and milk onto the egg yolk mixture and stir together. Then pass the mixture through a fine sieve into 6 ramekins.

Place the ramekins in a roasting tin, and pour in enough warm water to come half way up the sides of the ramekins – this will help the brûlées to cook evenly. Carefully transfer the tin to the oven and cook the brûlées for 40–50 minutes until set. Remove from the oven, take the ramekins out of the water and leave them to cool.

When cool, place them in the fridge to get completely cold. When the brûlées are cold and you're ready to serve, sprinkle them with caster sugar and caramelise using a blowtorch.

Serve when the caramel is cold and guests can crack through the topping.

HERB CRUST

*Make 250g, enough
for up to 14 portions*

This is a wonderfully savoury, herb-flecked butter that adds a crunchy texture and lots of flavour to all sorts of meat and fish. Try it top of a piece of poached fish, flashed under the grill, or mould it onto raw chicken and let it cook in the oven, basted in the butter.

200g softened unsalted
butter
200g white breadcrumbs
70g flat-leaf parsley,
chopped
30g chives, chopped
30g tarragon, chopped
1 garlic clove, finely
chopped
30g Cheddar cheese,
grated
salt and freshly ground
black pepper

Combine all the ingredients in a blender or food-processor and blitz until smooth and green. Tip the mixture onto a sheet of greaseproof paper, place another sheet over the top, and roll it out to a thickness of about 4mm. Store in the fridge until you need it.

You can cut the crust into any shape you need to cover meat or fish before cooking. And the mixture freezes well for up to a month.

MINT SAUCE

*Makes enough
for 1 meal*

I love mint sauce, not only because it's the classic British accompaniment to lamb (though I should point out that, in my opinion, the lamb has got to be Welsh) but because of the way it tastes. Beyond its mintiness, it's sharp and sweet: a British agrodolce. This recipe needs the freshest mint you can find.

6 tablespoons chopped
mint
3 tablespoons white
sugar
200ml malt vinegar

Place the mint and sugar in a bowl. Pour on 3 tablespoons boiling water and leave to stand until it's cold. Stir in the vinegar and leave it to stand for 1 hour. Serve at once – this is not a sauce that keeps.

PESTO

Makes 6–8 portions

Pesto is an Italian classic. It originates in Genoa, but its roots may be even older. The Romans used to blend herbs and cheese together to make a dish called 'moretum'. Everything was crushed together in a mortar (hence the name) to make an ancient, herbier version of something like Boursin cheese. This one is the perfect summer pasta sauce.

400g basil leaves
70g pine nuts, toasted
100g Parmesan cheese,
    grated
1 garlic clove, peeled
400ml good olive oil
salt and freshly ground
    black pepper

Combine the basil leaves, toasted pine nuts, Parmesan cheese and garlic clove in a blender or food-processor with a pinch of salt and a pinch of black pepper. Blitz until it's smooth – about 4–5 seconds. Don't over-work it – which is 'chef' for don't get too carried away – otherwise, you'll lose the colour of the basil.

Scrape the basil from the sides of the blender, then pour in the olive oil. Now pulse the blender until the mixture comes together – it should only take 5 seconds. Serve stirred into al dente linguine.

Bryn's Tip: If you want to make this to store, spoon your pesto into a sterilised jar (see the method on page 220) and, once it's settled, pour 1cm olive oil over the top so that it's well covered. The pesto will keep in the fridge for up to a month. This tip works just as well for the Wild Garlic Pesto on page 206.

WILD GARLIC PESTO

Makes 6–8 portions

Wild garlic has such a short season, so it's well worth picking some to make this rich and vibrant version of a traditional pesto sauce. It's delicious on pasta, and it goes very well with the Potato Salad on page 140.

400g wild garlic leaves
200g baby spinach
140g pine nuts, toasted
100g Parmesan cheese,
   grated
600ml good olive oil
salt and freshly ground
   black pepper

Put the wild garlic leaves, baby spinach, toasted pine nuts and Parmesan into a blender or food-processor with a pinch of salt and a pinch of black pepper and blitz it together very quickly.

Scrape the leaves from the sides of the blender and pour in the olive oil. Pulse again until it comes together – no more than 5 seconds. Chill the pesto to preserve its colour, and serve as soon as possible.

DRINKS

I couldn't let another book pass without having a section on drinks – alcoholic and non-alcoholic – that can be made from nature's own harvest, some sugar, water and a little patience.

Remember to sterilise your bottles by following the method on page 220.

BLACKCURRANT CORDIAL

Makes 1.2 litres

You may think it's a little odd to freeze the blackcurrants before turning them into a cordial, but it's exactly the same thinking that underlies the pressing of frozen grapes to make eiswein: the sugars and other solids in the fruit don't freeze, while the water inside it does, concentrating the juices. So it's well worth taking the time to do it.

1kg ripe blackcurrants, preferably frozen overnight, then defrosted
450g caster sugar
juice of ½ lemon

Put the defrosted blackcurrants, sugar and lemon juice in a blender and blitz well. Then pour the mixture into a muslin-lined colander set over a bowl. Fold the muslin over the mixture and place a light weight on top to help press out the liquid. Leave in the fridge overnight.

Taste the cordial for sweetness and adjust if it needs more sugar. Then pour into a clean container and store in the fridge. It will keep for 5–7 days, or you can freeze it.

To serve, dilute 1 part of the blackcurrant cordial with 2 parts of water.

HOMEMADE LEMONADE

Makes 1 litre

The Americans say 'When life gives you lemons, make lemonade.' While, sometimes, I might be tempted to change that advice to include the Lemon Tart on page 195, I enjoy a glass of homemade lemonade as much as the next bloke. It's fresh and refreshing – perfect on a hot day.

zest and juice of 3 unwaxed lemons
sprig of lemon thyme
170g sugar
300ml still water
700ml sparkling water, chilled

Put the lemon zest, juice, lemon thyme and sugar in a bowl. Mix well, then pour in the still water. Cover the bowl and leave to steep overnight, stirring occasionally if you can. When ready, strain the mix through a fine sieve into a clean jug, then pour in the chilled sparkling water.

Bryn's Tip: Adults can always add a slug of gin or vodka.

SLOE GIN

Makes about 1 litre

I love to cook with game so, come the autumn, whenever I go home to Wales, I'll often go shooting with my father and my Uncle Arwyn. While there's nothing better than coming back with a brace of pheasant for the pot, the things that make these afternoons are the conversations we have afterwards over a tot of sloe gin. There's nothing better to keep out the cold.

500g sloes
225g white sugar
gin, to cover

Prick the tough skins of the sloes all over with a clean needle, then put them in a sterilised jar (see the method on page 220). Add the sugar, then pour in enough gin just to cover, making sure you have a gap of about 3cm at the top. Seal the jar then shake well. Leave to stand in a cool dry place for 2 months, shaking the jar every 5–7 days.

When it's ready, pass the sloe gin through a fine sieve. Then pour it into clean bottles, sterilised by following the method on page 220, and seal.

UNCLE ARWYN'S BLACKBERRY VODKA

Makes about 1 litre

My Uncle Arwyn has been making this for about as long as I can remember. There's always a flask of it around when we go shooting.

1.1kg blackberries
1 bottle of vodka
100g sugar

Put the blackberries in a large container (we use a bucket!). Bash the berries with the end of a rolling pin, then add the sugar and the vodka. Mix well, then pour the mixture into 2 separate Kilner jars. Seal with the lids, and leave to stand in a cool dry place. Shake the jars every 5–7 days.

Taste after 1 month and if you think it needs more sugar, add a little extra at this point. Leave for a further month.

When ready, pass the vodka through a fine sieve. Pour the vodka into clean bottles, sterilised by following the method on page 220, and seal.

BASICS

Some of the recipes in this book require certain components you need to make yourself, none of them that demanding. Quite a few of them you can buy in the shops, but it's always better to make your own if you can. That way, you can control the various elements of seasoning – salt, pepper, acidity, sweetness, and so on. I've decided to collect those recipes together here. Most of them keep well, and I've made sure I tell you which ones freeze or for how long they'll keep in the fridge.

BARA BRITH

Serves 8

I published this recipe in my last book, and I make absolutely no apologies for including it again. As far as I'm concerned, there is only one recipe for Bara Brith – my Nain's (that's Welsh for gran). And this is it. It has been sustaining the Williams family for generations. And it predates thermostat ovens: when I asked Nain about the cooking times and temperatures for her Bara Brith, she said she didn't know. When I asked how come, she replied: 'Well, on a Tuesday, we'd bake the bread first, then the Bara Brith, then a rabbit pie. And when it cooled down, we might have done a rice pudding too.' Traditional Welsh cooking at its finest.

30g fresh yeast
  OR 2 x 7g sachets of
  easy-blend dried yeast
450ml warm water
900g plain flour,
  plus extra for dusting
120g brown sugar
120g lard, cut into
  small dice
350g currants
60g candied peel,
  finely sliced

Line a 900g loaf tin with greaseproof paper and preheat the oven to 180°C/gas mark 4.

If you're using fresh yeast, dissolve it in the lukewarm water; if you're using easy-blend dried yeast, mix it well with the dry ingredients. Mix all the dry ingredients together in a large bowl with the lard, and make a well in the centre with your hands. Then pour in the water.

Gradually work the flour into the water with your fingertips, until all the liquid has been absorbed, and you have a cohesive dough. It should feel smooth, not crumbly or ragged.

Turn the dough onto a well-floured surface and knead it for a good 5 minutes until it's shiny, smooth, silky and elastic.

Work the Bara Brith into a long sausage shape that will fit in the loaf tin.
Place in the tin and leave, covered with a tea towel, in a warm place until it has doubled in size. It should take about an hour or so.

Bake it in the oven for 40 minutes or until it's golden all over.

Serve for tea, spread with salty butter, or use in the pudding recipe on page 185.

RED WINE DRESSING

Makes 400ml

This is a classic salad dressing, given a shot of extra depth with rich sherry vinegar.

50ml red wine vinegar
50ml sherry vinegar
200ml olive oil
100ml vegetable oil
salt and freshly ground
   black pepper

Pour the vinegars into a bowl, season with salt and pepper, then whisk in the two oils. This will keep in the fridge for up to a month.

MUSTARD DRESSING

Makes about 350ml

Sharp and tangy, with the mellow, appley finish of cider vinegar: I love this dressing.

50ml cider vinegar
1 tablespoon
   grainy mustard
200ml olive oil
100ml vegetable oil
salt and freshly ground
   black pepper

Pour the vinegar into a bowl, season with salt and pepper, then whisk in the mustard and the two oils. This will keep in the fridge for up to a month.

TRUFFLE VINAIGRETTE

*Makes 200ml/
4–6 servings*

Decadent but very delicious.

100ml red wine
20ml red wine vinegar
50ml truffle oil
200ml olive oil
1 small black truffle
salt and freshly ground
   black pepper

Place the red wine into a saucepan over a high heat and reduce to one-third of its volume. Remove the pan from the heat and add the vinegar. Whisk in the truffle and olive oils. Season with salt and pepper, then grate in the truffle.

ODETTE'S HOUSE DRESSING

Makes about 1.2 litres

This is our absolute must-have dressing at Odette's. With the addition of fiery English mustard and white peppercorns, it's fairly robust, and gives salads a real boost. The blitzing of the ingredients means it emulsifies to a silky consistency. Keep in a sealed container in your fridge, ready for your next salad.

1 litre vegetable oil
20g salt
1 tablespoon white peppercorns, lightly cracked
1 shallot, peeled and chopped
200ml white wine vinegar
50g Dijon mustard
50g English mustard

Mix all the ingredients together in a large bowl, cover and place in the fridge. Leave for 24 hours.

Using an immersion blender, blitz the mixture until smooth, then pass through a fine sieve.

This will keep in the fridge for up to a month.

SPICED TOMATO CHUTNEY

Makes about 600ml

With cheese, cold meats or as an addition to sauces and stews, this is as handy a jar of pickle as you will ever have.

130ml malt vinegar
140g brown sugar
2 tablespoons tomato purée
2 teaspoons salt
1 teaspoon chilli powder
1 teaspoon ground ginger
1kg plum tomatoes, peeled (see page 144), deseeded and roughly chopped

Put all the ingredients except the tomatoes in a large heavy-based saucepan and bring to the boil over a medium heat. Add the chopped tomato and simmer very gently for 30–40 minutes, stirring occasionally to prevent sticking, until the mixture thickens and becomes jammy.

Remove from the heat and ladle into clean jars, sterilised by following the method on page 220. Label the jars with the date you made it. The chutney will keep for up to 6 months in the fridge.

PEA STOCK

Makes about 1.5 litres

Full of natural sweetness, we cook all our peas in this stock at Odette's. It is so simple to make, and it uses up the pods that would otherwise be thrown away or composted.

1kg pea pods
sprig of thyme
sprig of mint
big pinch of salt
big pinch of sugar

Place all the ingredients in a large saucepan. Cover with cold water and bring to the boil over a high heat. Reduce the heat and simmer for 20 minutes. Remove from the heat and pass through a fine sieve into a clean jug. Set aside to cool.

Bryn's Tip: This freezes very well, or you can keep it covered in the fridge for up to 5 days.

STOCK SYRUP

Makes about 300ml

Stock syrup is a really useful thing to have around. You can use it for a multitude of things. I use it in the Truffle and Pineapple Carpaccio on page 22.

250ml water
125g caster sugar

In a heavy based saucepan, bring the water and the sugar to the boil, whisking all the time until the sugar dissolves.

Once it comes to the boil, remove from the heat immediately and allow to cool. When it's cold, place it in a covered container in the fridge – the syrup should be cold when you use it.

SHORTCRUST PASTRY

*Makes enough to line
a 23cm tart tin*

Rich, buttery and short, this is the perfect pastry – I promise!

250g plain flour
125g unsalted butter,
    straight from the fridge,
    cut into small dice
pinch of salt
pinch of sugar
1 free range egg
1 tablespoon milk

Rub the flour and butter together using your fingertips until you have the texture of breadcrumbs. Add the salt and sugar. Then add the egg, and mix together. Finally add the milk and mix to form a dough. Remove from the bowl, wrap in clingfilm and set aside to rest in the fridge for 4 hours before using.

Bryn's Tip: You can freeze this once you've wrapped it in clingfilm.

SWEET PASTRY

*Makes enough to line
a 23cm tart tin*

A classic, rich, slightly sweetened shortcrust pastry.

250g plain flour
150g cold, unsalted butter
½ teaspoon salt
75g caster sugar
1 free range egg
1 free range egg yolk

Mix the flour, butter, salt and sugar together in the bowl of an electric mixer fitted with a paddle attachment. Then add the eggs and egg yolk and bring the dough together very quickly. Remove from the bowl, wrap in clingfilm and set aside in the fridge to rest for 4 hours before using.

HOW TO STERILISE JARS & BOTTLES FOR PICKLES & PRESERVES

It is very important to sterilise your jars before bottling your preserves. Likewise, if you're making my Sloe Gin or Blackberry Vodka, you need to sterilise the bottles. These are my easy methods.

Wash your jars and their lids in warm, soapy water. Rinse in fresh hot water and place upside down on a clean tea towel to dry. Pour some water in a large, deep pan and bring to the boil. Put the jars and lids in the pan and boil or simmer them for 10 minutes. Remove them using kitchen tongs, being careful not to touch the insides of the jars with your fingers. Set aside to steam dry.

Alternatively, put the clean jars and lids into the dishwasher and run it on the hottest cycle without using any soap. Remove them with kitchen tongs, being careful not to touch the insides of the jars with your fingers. Set aside to steam dry.

ACKNOWLEDGEMENTS

Thanks to all at Kyle Books and for Kyle's continued support.

Big thanks to Kay for all of your hard work and making head or tail of my recipes.

Thanks to Annie, Rosie and Wei for all your work on the book – a great team effort.

Thanks to Andy for all of the amazing photos.

Thanks to Dave, Jamie and the team at Odette's for pushing on while I was working on the book and to Fiona for juggling the dates and making sure I was at the right place at the right time.

And finally, thanks to Alan and Lisa at Aboud Creative for bringing the book alive.

INDEX